READ
MY BOOK

18 November, 2021

To Bill,

Wishing you only the GOOD !

READ MY BOOK

It's All About Me
(Good, Bad, and Ugly)
My Personal Reality

SETH S. SCHURMAN, M.D.

Acknowledgement

This has been an arduous project lasting over two years. I would like to thank two special people who gave their time to help me develop my writing skills and for proofreading my manuscript. First, I would like to thank my uncle, Ralph Glickman, who was an Attorney for the Armed Forces. He was a truly brilliant man with a lot of patience, spending hours every week to help me develop my writing skills. Without his dedication and faith in me, I would not have been able to create MY story. I am deeply indebted to him.

Also, I would like to thank my daughter, Kim, who proofread my manuscript and provided input to polish the finished product

I also would like to thank all the people in my life who helped me to advance and develop into the person I am today.

I had a truly wonderful life and I look forward too many more exciting adventures.

Abe and Bea

Dedication

I would like to dedicate this book to my parents,

Abe (Abraham) and Bea (Beatrice) Schurman.

They were in my mind the greatest parents that ever lived. They were a great inspiration and motivator for everything I accomplished. They were there for every step of my upbringing. They motivated me in so many ways to become the best person I could be. I was so very lucky to have them both to support me in the times of need, and furnish all the tools necessary to become successful in life.

They raised two future physicians, and they were very proud of that accomplishment.

I loved them and miss them so very much.

Contents

Introduction — i

Prologue — iii

Prologue Extension — vii

Chapter 1
Pail and shovel — 1

Chapter 2
Melody Country Club — 3

Chapter 3
Baron Teen Tours — 17

Chapter 4
Long Branch, New Jersey — 32

Chapter 5
Asbury Park, New Jersey — 45

Chapter 6
The Early Years — 55

Chapter 7
High School and College — 98

Chapter 8
Medical School — 109

Chapter 9
Residency and Fellowship — 142

Chapter 10
Marriage and Honeymoon — 170

Chapter 11
Air Force — 190

Chapter 12
Lessons Learned — 200

Illustrations — 204

About the Author — 208

Introduction

Why did I write this book? I have asked this question of myself many times. I suppose it fulfills an inner need to relive my life from its very beginning, with all the trials and tribulations that encompass it. I am able to remember all of the good times as well as the bad times. At my present age of 74, it is better to put it all in writing to preserve the memories that have enabled me to evolve into the person I am today. As I grow older, those memories will be preserved in detail, so that I can review what I wrote and prevent those memories from fading over time. More importantly, my children will be able to see what my life was like and to understand who I really am.

For most of my adult life I was always being told that it was all about me. Finally, I decided to write this book which IS ALL ABOUT ME. Now, everybody can read through these pages and discover what I was all about, what experiences I had, and get some idea about the real me. My mind is an open book, so this is the perfect vehicle to finally purge my memory and expose everything I can remember about ME. Personally, I think it is an interesting read and I hope you enjoy it too.

Every life has a beginning and an end. A lot of what I experienced was very funny, there are many passages that detail things that my dear wife and children helped in making my life as enjoyable and exciting as anyone could imagine. I will always be in awe of their excitement and curiosity of life that have made my journey so exciting and wonderful. After 48 years of marriage, I am still madly in love with my wife and I am excited about what our futures will hold. I want to create more memories with her together side by side.

So, fasten your seat belts and hold on tight for my amazing journey.

I envision this book to be followed by another one or two, to include my life experiences after serving in the United States Air Force.

Prologue

I was born on August 29, 1945 at Passaic General Hospital in Passaic, New Jersey. My mother was a homemaker and my father an Architect and General Contractor. I am of Russian descent with three of my grandparents emigrating from Minsk and Pinsk in Russia. My mother's mother was born in New York state, but both her parents were Russian immigrants as well.

I had one brother who was two years older than I was. He was a Physician specializing in Family Practice and Physiatry.

We moved to Paterson, New Jersey when I was very young and I remained there until I entered Medical School at the age of twenty. Upon completion of medical school, I moved to Brooklyn, New York, where I completed a Medical Internship, two years of Internal Medicine Residency, and a two-year Allergy Fellowship Program. It was there that I met my wife Jeanette. We married when I was 26 years old.

I was drafted into the Air Force after completion of my specialty training and served as Chief of Allergy at Keesler Air Force Base in Biloxi, Mississippi for a two - year period.

I started my practice, specializing in Allergy & Immunology in Fort Myers, Florida on July, 11, 1977, and continue in active practice today. My medical practice remains an exciting part of my life. I get an immense amount of pleasure investigating and solving the problems presented to me. The motivation to keep practicing is that I meet so many new patients and the challenge to help them gives me so much pleasure. I am very lucky in many ways. I have not missed a single day of work due to illness in many years, and I attribute that to luck and good genetics.

My approach to writing this book is to start from the beginning and devoting each chapter to a single life altering experience. I am going to be as accurate as I can and hopefully not miss anything important.

No one person up to this point knows everything, but now everybody will know everything. You might say that MY MIND will now be an open book.

Childhood Home

Prologue Extension

I will describe to you my grandparents and how our family surname became Schurman. I was very fortunate to know all of my grandparents.

My maternal grandfather was named Samuel. He was a tailor and owned his own business in downtown Paterson, until he lost everything to a fire. He was NOT insured. This led to an early retirement. Growing up around him, I was always given his advice on clothing coordination and fit and was constantly reminded of his profession. There was one thing about him that made me very unhappy and resulted in my not enjoying sports games especially baseball. He lived upstairs in the same house I lived in and was a baseball fanatic that would stay glued in front of his television set all day. He would refuse to interact with anybody whenever he was watching the games. I would visit him frequently but was never able to talk to him. To this day I refuse to watch any sports games being broadcast. Thank you, grandpa. He passed away a couple of weeks prior to my medical school graduation in 1970.

My maternal grandmother was named Rose. She was a homemaker and raised my mother and her brother. She suffered from metastatic cancer and passed before her husband. I will never forget the night she passed away. She was admitted to the hospital to have cataract surgery which was a common practice at that time. I went to visit her that night. As I was about to say good night, she called me back into the hospital room and told me something that is permanently imbedded in my mind. To this day, I do not know what prompted her out of a clear blue sky to tell me that I would meet a very nice girl, fall in love and get married. I was quite young at that point and was still in high school. Her premonition rang true when I first set my eyes on the most beautiful, intelligent girl I ever dated. It was truly love at first sight and that love continues now over 48 years later. How did she know? I was the last family member to see her alive prior to her passing.

My paternal grandfather was named Isaac. He was a successful general contractor. I was never able to talk to him because he never spoke English. My father was our interpreter. He was 76 years old upon his passing in 1953 on Halloween eve. I was only 8 years old at that time. Most interesting was the fact my father passed away also on Halloween at age 83 at 3:00 P.M. To this day, Halloween makes me depressed.

My paternal grandmother was also named Rose. She was a homemaker raising 4 sons and 2 daughters. She also did not speak any English but we were able to communicate through my father. Near the end, I started to teach her English on a weekly basis. She was able to learn, although was never able to form sentences. She was a remarkable cook and created the most delicious apple strudel in sheet form for the entire family frequently. To this day, I can still taste it, and have never found anything that was that good. I miss that more than anything. Whenever I visited her, she went to a drawer and took out a bag of Hershey's Kisses and would treat me to them. It amazes me the things we remember. She passed away at 95 years of age and remained alert to the very end. Near the end, she would ask me if I would remember her after her passing and I assured her I would. I will never forget that moment.

Now I will relate to you how a got my surname Schurman.

When my paternal grandfather arrived from Russia into the United States via Ellis Island, his name was Russian, and the spelling of it was very difficult. He met a man who told him that it should be changed to something more American and suggested the spelling that would ultimately be "Schurman".

The most unusual thing happened when my wife and I visited Prince Edward Island many years later. At that time a car ferry took you to that island. It was replaced by a bridge years later. As we drove on to the island, we noticed that everything was named "Schurman", (i.e. Schurman cottages, Schurman restaurant, Schurman department store). It completely surprised us. How could that be? Also, one thing that we will never forget was a large truck making a delivery to a department store. My wife's maiden name is Diamond. The truck making the delivery was labeled Diamond and the store labeled Schurman. Unbelievable.

When returning home, I discussed this with my father. He told me that his father arrived on Ellis Island, and met the man who suggested the new spelling. That man was from Prince Edward Island. What an unbelievable true story!

William Schurman

William Schurman (ca 1743 – September 15, 1819) was a businessman and politician of Prince Edward Island. He was a member of the Legislative Assembly of Prince Edward Island from 1785 to 1787.

He was born in New Rochelle, New York, the son of Jacob Schureman, of Dutch descent, and Jane Parcot, of Huguenot descent. In 1768, he married Jane Bonnet. Schurman married Elizabeth Hyatt in 1778.

Schurman remained loyal to Britain during the American revolution and, in 1783, immigrated to Tryon on St. John's Island (later Prince Edward Island). He settled at Bedeque the following year, setting up a store in his house and engaging in trade with a ship that he owned.

Besides serving in the colony's assembly, he was also a justice of the peace and overseer for roads. After losing his ship in 1799, Schurman became involved in shipbuilding. In 1808, he bought a wooded area along the Wilmot River, constructed a sawmill and entered into the trade in lumber. He died at his home in the Wilmot Valley in 1819.

His great-grandson Jacob Gould Schurman later became president of Cornell University and an American ambassador.

External links

- Biography at the *Dictionary of Canadian Biography Online* (http://www.biographi.ca/009004-119.01-e.php?&id_nbr=2650)

Prince Edward Island

Another interesting fact.

When my grandfather arrived on Ellis Island, he filled out a form required by the Bureau of Immigration and Naturalization. The form was titled a Declaration of Intention, in which he was required to renounce forever all allegiance and fidelity to any foreign prince, potentate, state, or sovereignty, and particularly to Nicholas II Emperor of Russia of which I am now a subject. He also denied he was an anarchist, that he was not a polygamist, nor a believer in the practice of polygamy. I have a copy of the original document signed and dated by him on November 9, 1907, copy attached.

My first name was chosen in memory of a family member who was shot down by enemy fire during World War 2. Also, most people do not know that "Seth" was the third son of Adam in the bible.

BUREAU OF IMMIGRATION AND NATURALIZATION
DIVISION OF NATURALIZATION

DECLARATION OF INTENTION

(Invalid for all purposes seven years after the date hereof)

State of New Jersey ss: In the *Common Pleas* Court
Passaic County of *Passaic County*

I, *Isaac Schurman*, aged *30* years,
occupation *Mason & Plasterer*, do declare on oath ~~affirm~~ that my personal
description is: Color *White*, complexion *Dark*, height *5* feet *4* inches,
weight *144* pounds, color of hair *Brown*, color of eyes *Brown*
other visible distinctive marks *None*
: I was born in *Minsk Russia*
, on the *10th* day of *March*, anno
Domini 1*877*; I now reside at *16 Vreeland Ave Passaic NJ*
I emigrated to the United States of America from *Rotterdam Netherlands*
on the vessel *Nordam*; my last
foreign residence was *Minsk Russia*
It is my bona fide intention to renounce forever all allegiance and fidelity to any foreign
prince, potentate, state, or sovereignty, and particularly to *Nicholas II*
Emperor of Russia, of which I am now a ~~citizen~~ subject; I
arrived at the port of *New York*, in the
State ~~Territory~~ ~~District~~ of *New York* on or about the *5th* day
of *October*, anno Domini 1*904*; I am not an anarchist; I am not a
polygamist nor a believer in the practice of polygamy; and it is my intention in good faith
to become a citizen of the United States of America and to permanently reside therein:
SO HELP ME GOD.

Isaac Schurman
(Original Signature of Declarant.)

Subscribed and sworn to ~~affirmed~~ before me this *9th*

[SEAL.]

day of *November*, anno Domini 19*07*

Declaration of Intention

CHAPTER 1
Pail and shovel

To begin with, I will not deceive you by telling you that I remember taking my first breath. Actually, my very first recollection was an episode I had with a female playmate. Her name is Rona Miller and to this day we are in direct communication.

We were both very young, maybe 4 or 5 years old, about 68 years ago. She was a school mate and on one memorable occasion, we were playing in the dirt in front of my house. She had a shovel, but I had a PAIL and shovel. She wanted my pail, but I didn't want to give it to her, so she took the female prerogative and forcibly took it away from me. That angered me, so I did what I thought was acceptable, and hit her over the head with the shovel. She started crying and screaming, and my parents were not happy, so I was punished. I don't think we ever played again together in the dirt. It was a smart decision on her part.

To this day on each of our birthdays, we bring up that episode. It is indelibly engraved in our psyche.

Another interesting fact. We both graduated from Eastside High School in Paterson, New Jersey in January, 1963. I was the tallest in the graduating class and she was the shortest. It was only appropriate that we were selected to be Mutt and Jeff, and our picture is in our yearbooks. How funny is that?

CHAPTER 2
Melody Country Club

Brill and Gretenstein

I must admit that I had a wonderful childhood. I was spoiled and my father was a strict disciplinarian. It was the best of both worlds! From my earliest memories we spent most of our summers in Liberty, New York at the Melody Country Club in the Borscht Belt, in its hay day. The hotel was owned by the Brill and Gretenstein family. Harry Gretenstein was a taxi driver in New York City during the winter months, and jointly operated the hotel during the summer with Hy Brill, and

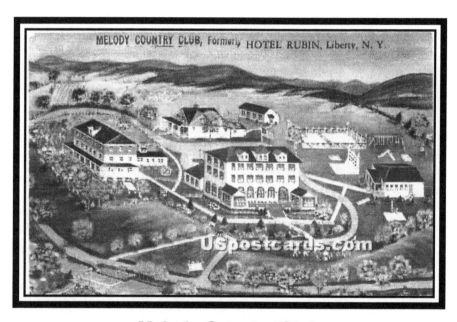

MELODY COUNTRY CLUB, Formerly HOTEL RUBIN, Liberty, N. Y.

Melody Country Club

his parents. Hy was a man of all trades, not only helping operate the hotel but also held a franchise installing pin ball and other gaming machines in a number of hotels upstate.

I would spend the entire summer each year at this hotel, which is full of great memories. I learned how to swim there at age 15. Several years later the hotel was sold to a group that holds summer camp for girls. That pool exists to this day and can be found on google maps.

My father would work in the city and arrive late on Friday for two nights each weekend. I was excited to see him visit, not so much for the fact we were separated but more due to the fact he would bring me comic books weekly to read. In fact, I learned to read from all of those comic books which dated back to the 1940's, and were priced at only $0.10 per copy. Specifically, I read all the original superman and batman comics. I had a very large collection and I saved every copy, never throwing or giving any of them away. I stored them in 2 large cardboard boxes in the basement of our home. After I moved to Chicago to attend medical school, my parents moved to Sussex, New Jersey, and in the process of the move threw both boxes away without asking me. To this day, I cannot forgive them for what they did. I suppose they thought the comics were old and worthless, which is not true now. OH WELL, water under the bridge.

As I commented before, Hy Brill was a man of many trades and one of them was breaking wild horses. The Hotel consisted of the main hotel and smaller buildings to house guests. There was a parking lot in the center of the complex. One day, Hy took a series of cars and formed a large central space in which to break a wild horse (similar to rallying wagons in the old days to fight Indians). As everybody watched through the hotel windows and behind the cars, Hy brought in the wild horse and mounted it. That horse fought with all of its might to get Hy off of its back to no avail. It was beyond belief and the most memorable thing I had ever seen! It seemed to go on forever, but eventually the horse conceded defeat and relinquished control to Hy. I replay that episode many times in my mind.

My father enjoyed target practice with a single 22 caliber rifle. As I got older, he would take me out and teach me how to handle the gun. I mastered it over time. Harry also had a liking for guns. I remember vividly the time he brought a German Luger to use for target practice. Harry was a small man in stature and very thin. We watched as he loaded the gun and stood back when he fired it. The recoil from the gun knocked him to the ground. I clearly remember that moment.

Most fascinating of all was the fact my father was obsessed with cameras. He had a wind up 16mm movie camera and took loads of pictures. Prior to his death and unbeknownst to me, he transferred a lot of film to a CD to give to me. It contained pictures I had never seen or known he had taken including a video of me shooting the rifle. Amazing footage! I have that wind up camera to this day on my desk.

The hotel was located in farm country with a lot of acreage with many family owned farms nearby. We would visit one of the dairy farms on the nearby hill and it was there that we learned to milk cows. We also drank milk directly from the cow which was a very thick, rich, and creamy milk. It had a very unique taste and it was still warm. At that age, little did we know about Brucellosis, and luckily, we did not contract any milk borne diseases.

We also used to collect blueberries and blackberries which grew wild in the fields. We would bring them back to the hotel to the kitchen to be served to the guests. There were a lot of green crab apple trees nearby and we collected them as well. I will attest to the fact they were more bitter than a regular apple, and a very strong laxative.

Let me now tell you about the giant bull-frogs. Richie, the owner's son, my brother, and I decided one day to catch some large bullfrogs. The largest I have ever seen. We decided to place three of them in three large empty coffee cans and covered them with lids with holes to allow them to breathe. We placed them in the hall outside our hotel room on the second floor. Early the next morning there were screams coming from the hotel lobby beneath us. The frogs had escaped and headed to the lobby. The women were screaming when they saw them. We were able to catch all three again and were forced to let them go. Of course, our respective parents were very angry and we were punished.

Hy Brill loved to go fishing at sunrise at the Never-sink Reservoir. Richie, my brother, and I would get up at 4AM since the fish were easier to catch early in the morning. We would fish for a few hours and most times we did not catch anything. People say that patience is a virtue. In this case it was boring and agonizing, getting up that early without a single catch. Since that time, fishing is something I deliberately avoid doing. As an interesting side-note, we needed bait to go fishing and we would collect live worms as bait. Richie discovered an easy way to collect the worms (night crawlers) from the worm holes where they were all hiding. He formulated a mustard solution, and then poured it into the worm holes. The worms would literally come flying out of the holes and we easily collected them. It was sadistic thinking back. BOYS WILL BE BOYS.

Grossinger's Hotel was only a short distance from us. During the summer Rocky Marciano used the hotel for training sessions. We would hike to the hotel and watch him box. Quite a sight to see.

Directly across from the entrance to Grossingers was located the Triangle Diner. They served Chinese roast pork sandwiches on garlic bread which was the best sandwich I ever had and we ate there frequently. I will

Triangle Restaurant

never forget that taste! Nobody has been able to duplicate it and it is another food delicacy that I continue to search for. That specialty sandwich was created in the Borscht belt. It was a curiosity because it was a Jewish enclave with an abundance of Hassidic and Orthodox Jews. Eating pork was not allowed since it was a dietary restriction. However, I believe that they temporarily became un-orthodox while eating it. That was the last place on earth you would expect to serve that sandwich.

I learned how to drive at the age of 15, al-beit illegally, in a 1953 pale green Cadillac. I drove it frequently to and from the town of Liberty. My father took pictures of that car and it is on the CD he gave me. I took my driving test at age 17 in that car.

Those vacations at the hotel were so en-joyable! There was no air conditioning be-cause the mountain air at night was cool and refreshing. We would sleep with the windows open and at the break of dawn, the roosters would crow and wake us up. Also, at night there were millions of fire flies and we would collect them in bottles.

1953 Cadillac

One unique event occurred when the Russian's placed Sputnick in orbit around the earth. The night sky in the mountains was the blackest that could be found anywhere and all the celestial bodies were clearly displayed. One night all the hotel guests were told that Sputnick would be flying overhead and could easily be seen as a flashing light as it crossed the night sky. It was quite an experience!

Other unusual things we did, included trying to ride the cows and cow chip throwing contests. We also participated in apple juice drinking contests to see who could drink the most apple juice in one sitting. Life was good! I also remember asking my father for ten cents to buy mounds candy bars which to this day are my favorite. Inflation since then really increased the price dramatically.

There was one scary incident I will never forget. Richie, my brother, and I were playing in the woods. A sudden thunder and lightning storm developed and we started to run back to the safety of the hotel. Between the wooded area and the hotel was a large field which contained cows and bulls. The bulls were angry from the storm and they gave us very angry looks. We were seeking cover under a large tree. We had no choice but to run through the field. As soon as we left the tree there was a large flash of lightening with a very loud noise as it struck the tree that we were seeking shelter under. It literally split the tree in half. We were lucky to survive.

Two funny incidents occurred in the bungalows at the hotel. The first involved a blind maid who went to clean one of the rooms. She always knocked before entering each room and when she got no response, she entered the room and started to make up the bed. She then discovered a guest still sleeping in the bed. The other episode involved a maid entering another bungalow. Upon entering the building, she was attacked by a "monster" and she ran out of the building screaming. The "monster" ended up being a Pekinese dog, which does look frightening!

One summer, my father bought me a Daisy Pump BB rifle. I still have it and enjoyed shooting it. Little did I know that 30 years later, Mr. Hough, President of the Daisy Air Rifle Company would become a patient of mine in Naples, Florida for Allergy problems. I treated him for a few years before his passing.

One of the most painful experiences I had was on July fourth when we were playing with small fire crackers. We would hold them in one hand, light the fuse, and throw them before they exploded. I held one between my thumb and second digit, lit it, and before I could throw it, it exploded. The pain was excruciating! I soon lost all sensation in both digits and they both turned black. I was very lucky that I did not lose my fingers. The pain and numbness subsided several days later. Needless to say, I never did that again. A very painful learning experience!

Another painful experience involved my encounter with a wasp's nest. There was a concrete dam near the hotel and there was a wasp nest next to it. I stepped on it, not knowing it was there, and was promptly stung on my right ear lobe. The pain was excruciating with immediate swelling. Cold wet mud was applied to ease the pain and prevent further swelling.

Another funny episode occurred when my mother went to have her hair colored. Her best friends, Babs and Jack owned a hair salon. A few hours after the coloring, her hair turned green. It was the funniest thing we ever saw!

There was a large lake not far from the hotel. One evening at dusk, my brother, Richie, and I were rowing a boat when all of a sudden hundreds of bats came out of a nearby cave. They never tried to attack us. I never saw anything like it, it was scary.

My brother, Ritchie, and I were always taking long hikes. On one occasion, Ritchie decided we should hitch a ride to get back to the hotel. That was the first and last time I will ever do that. There we were, preteens thumbing cars for a ride. There were very few cars on this isolated back woods road. One car did stop to pick us up and it was one of the scariest experiences I ever had. As soon as we got in the car, the driver locked the doors and began to speed down this winding, hilly road. We were yelling for him to stop and let us out which he finally did and warned us to never again thumb a ride with anyone. He could have killed us and no one would ever know who did it. We all learned a valuable lesson.

CHAPTER 3
Baron Teen Tours

Train tour of the United States

In 1958, our parents sent us on a tour of the United States with a company called Baron Teen Tours. The trip lasted about four weeks and transportation was provided using trains. In some cities we stayed at hotels. We left from New York and our first stop was in New Orleans. Other stops included the states of Texas, Nevada, California, Arizona, and Illinois and a few other states.

We had tours at each stop with all meals included. There were a few memories that stand out in my mind. The train ride was quite an experience! In those days you heard a loud clickety clack as the train rode the tracks. It was continuous and monotonous and it took several weeks after the trip ended before that annoying noise left my head. Years later they developed better connectors between tracks and you no longer hear that annoying sound. We had numerous adventures and we took still and video tape of it all.

In New Orleans we rode the sternwheeler boat on the Mississippi River. There are massive dikes on each side of the river preventing flooding. We were on the boat looking down at the residential communities on both sides of the river. It was very strange looking down with the river being so high.

The French Quarter was really nice. The music, shops, restaurants, and of course, the street people. It was a unique first - time experience at the age of 13. I must not forget to mention Café Du Monde on the river with its heavily sugared beignets. It is still there and still as famous as ever.

Café Du Monde

Another stop was San Diego. We took buses to cross over into Mexico to see a Bull fight at the bull fighting ring located next to the Pacific Ocean. The seats are priced as to whether you were seated in the sunny side of the ring or the shady side. You can guess where we were seated during the summer in brutally hot Mexico.

We spent time walking around Tijuana unsupervised and it was an awakening for me. Such a dirty town with extreme poverty that you cannot imagine. The residents were bathing and washing clothes in the muddy river. Downtown there were numerous bars that had swinging wood doors like in the old west. We were able to look into these bars to see what went on. In one memorable bar, was a woman on the stage lying on her back. A donkey was brought in which mounted and had sex with her. Remember, I was innocent at the ripe old age of 13.

When we entered Mexico, we crossed a bridge on foot. There was a large dead dog lying on the bridge. When we went across the same bridge eight hours later, that dog was still there decaying on the bridge.

Bullring by the Sea

When we returned from Mexico, we visited the San Diego Zoo which was amazing to see.

In Los Angeles we visited Disney Land. We also took a day trip on a Hydrofoil boat to Santa Catalina Island about 45 minutes away. The one thing I remember most were the Flying Fish that surrounded the boat. They had fins that acted like wings and they would soar in the air over and over again. There must have been a million of them. When I took that same boat years later, the flying fish were gone because of pollution.

I had second cousins living in L.A. and their father was a film developer for major Hollywood movies. His best friend was a security guard at Universal Studios. At that time Gunsmoke was being filmed at the Studio. Unfortunately, I was there on a Saturday, when they were not filming. My cousin gave us a tour of the studio and the Gunsmoke set. It was exciting at my age to actually be there on that set. I never got to meet James Arness (Marshall Dillon), Chester, Doc, Miss Kitty , Festus and the others. The full set was built inside a large building (sound stage) and we visited the jail, saloon, etc. Of interest, when they showed people during filming drinking beer, it was REAL beer, since that was the only way to have the bubbles on top. We also visited the set of Pete and Gladys which was to start filming the next week. It was so strange being there and then seeing it on TV each week.

Las Vegas was amazing! Remember, I was there for the first time in 1960 at the age of 13. There was one main road entering and leaving the strip. At the northern end you entered downtown where it all began. At that time the strip consisted of a main road with a few scattered casino hotels, specifically the Sands, Flamingo etc. They each had huge brightly colored signs announcing their presence and the headliners who were appearing at each one. There was a concrete sidewalk alongside the road. The casinos were few and far between. In between the casinos was the desert stretching out for as far as you could see with tall mountains in the distance. They were selling desert land for $50.00 an acre. True, in 1960 $ 50.00 an acre was unbelievable. I wish I had had the money to buy it at that time.

Of course, at our age gambling was strictly forbidden, although we walked from casino

Las Vegas

to casino and managed to play some penny slots before being shown the exit. We also wanted to get autographs from some of the stars. I managed to meet, and to this day still have a book of autographs from Gene Barry, Jane Wyman, Jerry Colonna, and others.

I will never forget the intense heat we experienced there. They said you could fry an egg on the sidewalk and I believe it.

I was there when the iconic sign announcing your entrance to the strip was there.

The casinos downtown were clustered together within a few city blocks. There were low stakes gambling with penny and nickel slots. There were also a lot of sleazy bars, strip joints, and restaurants. The Vegas strip, in contrast, was a horse of a different color and was upper crust and lavish and had high end gambling, restaurants, accommodations, etc. In the lobby of these hotels they would serve free food. There were lines of people waiting their turn to get prime rib on buns and a variety of other delicious foods. I remember standing in line many times. The food was excellent! I don't remember having to pay for any meals while in town.

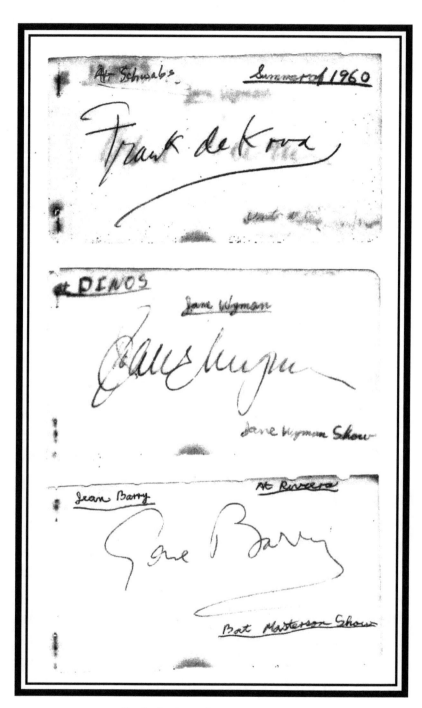

Celebrity Autographs

Celebrity Autographs

Now when I visit Vegas, it is beyond belief what it has turned out to be. I remember when I was there the first time. Who would imagine the growth and wealth that has amassed there? It was the number one growth center in the country for so many years, and it continues to develop.

In San Francisco, we rode the cable cars, rode down Lombard Street, the crookedest street in the world, and spent time in Chinatown. We also visited Alcatraz, Sausalito (the artist colony), and traveled across the Golden Gate Bridge by bus and foot.

I visited the Napa Sonoma valley and we took the wine train to the northern part of the valley where I visited the petrified forest. There was also a Geyser located at the northern end of Napa Valley in Calistoga that would erupt every twenty minutes or so releasing a plume of hot water. I was told that this was the only other active Geyser in the United States other than Old Faithful which is substantially larger in size.

I also visited the giant redwood trees north of San Francisco in Muir Woods, a beautiful national treasure with all types of wildlife and small rivers running through it. One thing I learned from the Park Ranger, was that the Redwood trees are the tallest trees in the world and there has never been a documented <u>natural death</u> of any of them. Acid rain has caused some to die. They are the oldest living plant species in the world.

I visited the Grand Canyon as well. We spent a couple of nights in Angel Camp in little log houses. The wildlife would visit the camp at night looking for food. They were very domesticated and not afraid of humans. One night an adult deer visited us with large furry antlers and it allowed us to pet him. One of us touched the furry antler, which is very sensitive, and the deer ran off. The sunrise and sunsets were spectacular over the canyon. I was sitting on a stone wall overlooking the canyon with my left hand resting on the wall. All of a sudden, I felt moisture on one of my fingers. When I looked to see what it was, I found a squirrel had my finger in its mouth and was sucking on it. Needless to say, I pulled it out immediately. I was lucky it didn't bite me.

I also visited Yosemite National Park, a must - see on every bucket list. In the evenings during the summer they had what they called a Fire Fall. On the top of one of the highest peaks they would light a fire and after sunset would push the red - hot embers off the top. It was a river of fire falling to the canyon floor. Absolutely gorgeous! Then, a few years, later because of fears of starting a forest fire, it was stopped. They now have a series of lights to try to create the actual thing. Very disappointing after seeing the original.

Fire Fall

CHAPTER 4
Long Branch, New Jersey

It was during this same time period in the early 1950s that I also frequently spent time at the Jersey shore. My father and his brother Aaron built several apartment complexes ocean front in Long Branch. To my knowledge these complexes were Mafia funded.

In my early years I was very clumsy and managed to get into some funny situations. This is one of the funniest. When the

Apartments

foundation was placed during construction, they apply stakes into the ground with heavy twine connecting them so that everything would line up, i.e. straight walls. When concrete was poured into the trenches, straw was used to cover up the wet cement to allow it to cure properly. I wanted to lend a hand in carrying straw to cover the concrete and I tripped over the twine and my entire body fell face down into the wet cement. I was coated with wet concrete from head to foot. My father was not happy and my mother was livid. At that time, we were staying at the beautiful Garfield Grant Hotel downtown with its gorgeous marble lobby. I obviously needed to be cleaned up and we needed to go through the main entrance of the hotel to get to our room. I clearly remember being totally humiliated as I walked through the lobby, dripping wet cement onto the marble lobby floor. Looking back, it was very funny, but at the time not so much.

Another vivid memory was that we used to spend hours on the beach under a very hot sun to develop sunburn. No-one knew about the sun causing skin cancer until many years later and sunscreen was first being introduced. We used to burn our skin red and

Garfield Grant Hotel

applied Calamine lotion to help cool it down. My brother and I then used to peel off strips of skin. At the time we never gave it a second thought. Looking back, that was very stupid because many people who sunburned developed skin cancer thirty or more years later. I have a yearly skin evaluation and, luckily, no cancer has developed yet.

Allow me to introduce a piece of history here. In the early 1950's Ocean Avenue in Long Branch was truly Ocean Avenue. It was a wide avenue with a median. To my memory there was a boardwalk, and a wide sandy beach. The apartments my father built were on Ocean Avenue directly across from the beach. There was a terrible hurricane that hit Long Branch and destroyed Ocean Avenue. The night the storm hit my Uncle Aaron was sleeping in an end unit of the apartment complex nearest the beach. My father and others were out watching the storm as it hit. Waves from the ocean were huge and took out the wide beach as well as Ocean Avenue. The waves were breaking on the roof of the complex. The apartments themselves survived that hurricane. The next morning, my uncle was told there were heavy rains. He never knew waves were breaking on the roof. The apartment complex survived the storm, and no one was injured.

After the storm passed a massive reconstruction was started and Ocean Avenue was relocated one block inland. The original Avenue was developed into a pedestrian walkway with benches and the beach was now extremely narrow. To prevent further erosion, jetties were installed using massive boulders to prevent future erosion.

I remember spending a lot of time on that beach. They put up ropes so that bathers could walk into the ocean and hold on for dear life. The waves were strong and everybody would venture out into the rough water. The water was frigid and it must have been 50 degrees or less during the summer months. I would shiver, my teeth would chatter, and my fingers and lips would turn blue because of the cold water. Now at my ripe old age, if the water in the pool is not at least 86 degrees I refuse to go into it. I still vividly remember the bone chilling cold. BRRRR. Why did I go into the water?? I was just young and stupid, but at the time at my young age it was a wonderful bone chilling experience.

There were two great restaurants on Ocean Avenue. The first one was called the Hollywood Restaurant which was owned by a cousin of ours. Basically, a soda fountain kind of place with great hamburgers. Just across the street diagonally on the ocean side was the famous Embers Restaurant which had the greatest hot dogs around. They used Schickhaus Hot Dogs, and they are still in business in Long Branch selling their hot dogs wholesale.

My father built and operated two large properties on the ocean in Long Branch. He built a large hotel with casino. The casino was unique in that the large round stage was on hydraulics and would rise out of the floor which was the first of its kind in New Jersey. I used to enjoy riding up and down as it rotated. I Never forgot that stage. When they had affairs there, a dwarf with a small round hat was walking around and selling Philip Morris cigarettes. As he walked around, he would yell out "CALL FOR PHILLIP MORRIS". My father told me that I wanted to play with him, thinking that he was my age.

Another memory is imbedded in my mind. The mafia helped finance the hotel. One day,

Schickhaus Hot Dog

my father was to meet one of the mob bosses in the lobby and I tagged along. The fellow he met was short and stocky with a hat and wore spats around his ankles. I will never forget that fellow. It's as if he walked out of a James Cagney movie. He spoke without moving his lips. He was the stereotypical mobster type.

In later years the hotel complex became a weight loss institute attracting a lot of celebrities. One of those who stayed there was Jack E. Leonard the comedian. They would serve special restrictive diets to help people lose weight. Jack would sneak across the street to my cousin's restaurant to fill himself with hamburgers and other foods. He never could curb his appetite.

The other property my father operated for several years was the Colony Surf Club down the road just before crossing a bridge to Deal, New Jersey. We had a lot of fun at that Club. The pastry chef at the club was named Smitty, and he made the most delicious cakes and pastries you could imagine. Each year on my birthday, he baked a multi-tiered cake just for me, very decorated and loaded with candles. He would roll it out poolside, and after lighting the candles everybody sang me "Happy

Colony Surf Club

Colony Surf Club

Birthday". Can you imagine a better way to celebrate one's birthday? They would sing it over a loud speaker system. I frequently in my mind flash back to that time. Smitty eventually left the club to work as a personal pastry chef for Arthur Godfrey.

The club had two enormous swimming pools side by side with large fountains. The water was frigid and it was very difficult getting into it. There were no heated pools back then.

My uncle Aaron purchased a large very old Victorian mansion nearby, something out of an Alfred Hitchcock movie. He called it Withering Heights. We used to play there frequently and at a very young age he let me sit in his lap and drive a car on the property. He applied the gas because my legs were not long enough to reach the peddles.

My father also built an addition to the Long Branch train station. I was there to see them work on it in the early 1950's.

When you left to drive to Asbury Park, you passed through the city of Deal, New Jersey. As I remember, the main road connecting the

Long Branch Train Station

two cities was made of cobblestone which made for quite a bumpy ride. Deal is a rich community with a lot of up-scale homes. One home in particular was a beautiful home painted in a rich coral color with white trim. Every time I saw it, I was in awe of the coloring. At that time, 60 years ago, I decided my home would be painted the same color. Not only did I live up to that promise, but I also painted one of my office buildings the same color. Both look stunning!

CHAPTER 5

Asbury Park, New Jersey

There are so many great memories of Asbury Park in its hay day. There was the wide boardwalk with seating overlooking a wide expanse of beach with the waves crashing ashore. We spent a lot of time on the beach getting our intense sunburns. Along the boardwalk were the large casinos where movies were shown and games were played including skeet-ball, pinball machines, and loads of other games you would find on a carnival fairway. As you

Boardwalk

played you would accumulate points, and when you were finished playing the points were redeemed for stuffed animals and other toys. Along the boardwalk were many gift shops and stands selling cotton candy, candied apples, salt water taffy, and other places for drinks. We also played miniature golf most evenings and rode the many carnival rides there. I can still smell the salt air from the ocean on light evening breezes along with the food being prepared. You had to be there to experience it real time. It is difficult to put it all into words. On the southern end of the boardwalk was a large merry-go-round which blasted carousel music and there was a chance to grab a ring. I rode that merry-go-round so many times! It was very exciting and a lot of fun. Here is another point of interest. On the merry-go-round there was one black horse which I rode. About ten years ago I went back to visit and rode it again, this time taking extensive video pictures on and off it. Then a year or two later it was closed down. I searched extensively on line to try to find where it was and to try and buy one of the horses from it to no avail. Then, it was revealed that an amusement park in Myrtle Beach purchased it and placed it in its park where it resides today. How wonderful is

Merry-go-round

that! I plan on going there someday to ride that horse again. It is on my bucket list.

Just across the street from the merry-go-round was Palace Amusements, which housed a tall Ferris wheel that I rode numerous times. Scary but fun, especially on windy evenings. I remember sitting in the gondola when I was at the highest point with the cool summer breezes and the wind blowing the gondola back and forth. The view, especially at night, was breathtaking. Tilly was the mascot painted at the entrance to the fun house. Inside was the hall of mirrors, a large revolving wheel you needed to navigate through, bumper cars, a haunted house, and more. So many fun things to do!

Nearby was a lake and there were motor boat rides and the Swan Boats.

All of this disappeared over the years as the demographics of the area changed, and there was no upkeep. It was like nobody cared and everyone just walked away. I understand there is a resurgence to rehabilitate and bring back what was there, but I honestly do not see that happening.

Palace Amusements

Swan Boats

The largest Hotel was the Berkeley – Carteret (1920) Hotel located directly across the street from the boardwalk. There was a large wide concrete pedestrian walkway for people to walk across to the beach and avoid street level traffic. It was on the second floor of the hotel. One year, the walkway collapsed onto the street. I do not remember if anybody got hurt. The hotel is still there today and is still open for business.

Another fixture was a large salt water swimming pool (Monte Carlo Pool) covering an entire city block. It was billed as the largest salt water pool in the world and it certainly was. I swam in it many times. They had baths and changing rooms. Every summer we spent time in the pool. And, every summer I developed Athlete's Foot from the changing rooms and would treat it daily with Desenex antifungal powder. Sometimes the infection was so bad, there would be severe scaling between the toes and bleeding. I still would do it over and over. You just need to take the good with the bad. There was a tunnel under Ocean Avenue connecting the pool to the beach. They placed a plastic wristlet on your wrist so that you could return to the pool after spending time on the beach. I can

Berkeley-Carteret Hotel

Monte Carlo Pool

still smell the musty mildew odor while inside that long dark tunnel. The pool no longer exists and was replaced with buildings.

Bruce Springsteen got his start in Asbury Park at the Stone Pony nightclub. Danny DeVito was also raised there and they both go back to visit.

The best restaurant to my memory was across a small bridge in the town of Belmar, New Jersey. It was called Dave and Evelyn's Seafood House. It was right on a river, with a seaman motif and it had a large salt water fish tank inside. The food was extraordinary! I knew Evelyn in the early days before she passed on. The restaurant is still there and my wife and I ate there a few years ago during a trip.

I had a great childhood!

The Stone Poney

Dave & Evelyn's Seafood

CHAPTER 6
The Early Years

In this chapter I am going to relive some of my transgressions which I am not proud of, and other interesting events.

My first boyhood friend of many years was Michael Gordon. He was more adventurous than I was and led both of us into some interesting situations.

Michael was interested in rockets and decided to build and fire them off with my help. He would buy hollow pipes and attach fins to the base of each. He then bought gun powder and somehow made a paste out of it and then attached a fuse. We would go to a nearby field and fire them off. Some would reach almost 40 feet.

Michael and I had another friend we used to play with. His name was Bruce. We both used to take advantage of him and one time got him into a perilous situation. About a block from where we lived in Paterson, New Jersey was a steel company. They were building an addition to their factory and were pouring concrete for footings for the foundation. Shortly after the workmen left, we decided to play there. I do not remember exactly how it happened, but Bruce ended up falling into the concrete feet first and started sinking into it. It was like quicksand but thank G-D we were able to pull him out before he became a permanent part of the building. It sounds funny now, but at the time scary as hell. Bruce stopped playing with us after that. Smart decision on his part.

One day Michael dreamed up an idea that would potentially make us a lot of money. He decided to make whipped cream and sell it to our neighbors. We went and purchased some heavy cream and placed it into a blender and added a lot of sugar. We whipped it into the consistency of whipped cream and went door to door to sell it. Unfortunately, none of it sold and we were left with a lot of unsold whipped cream that didn't really taste good. We should have stuck to selling lemonade!

What he thought up next was not nice. We were kids, so what would you expect? The street where we lived was poorly lit at night, so it attracted couples in cars to "make out". We were old enough to know what they were up to, so Michael decided to get a flash light and after watching one particular couple, he turned it on and directed it to their car. Obviously, the man got a little upset, got out of the car half-dressed and chased us for almost a block. Thank G-D we managed to escape. Again, very funny from our perspective!

Another episode occurred on the night of Halloween. Again, Michael came up with another neat idea. He wanted to get some fire crackers, place them in metal mail boxes, light them, and run away. The noise of them going off was so loud it echoed through the neighborhood! At one home, the firecrackers actually knocked the mailbox off the wall.

You will notice, I was innocent in everything that happened. I just followed along to see what would happen. I suffer NO guilt. You know what they say –Boys will be Boys.

I was raised in the Orthodox Jewish faith. Rabbi Tannenbaum operated his own Temple. In the Temple woman were required to sit apart from the men. The whole service was conducted in Yiddish. I never understood anything that was said and I sat there weekly until I was a Bar Mitzvah. I learned to read and pronounce it all, but what it was about I have no clue to this day. The best thing about weekly services was the breakfast that was served after we suffered through the service. I think the only reason I went weekly was for the most delicious bagels, lox, and cream cheese. The other reason I went was because my father made me. Ultimately, I think going to eat there was more motivating to me. He was raised Orthodox, and as mentioned before, neither of his parents spoke English.

I had a Bar Mitzvah ceremony at the age of 13. A rite of passage to manhood. The entire service was in Yiddish which I never understood a word of. I was required to read in Hebrew the entire time, from the Torah and a Hebrew book. Let me describe the room we were in, with a large congregation present. The Rabbi had marked places where I would read after the congregation read their parts. The Rabbi faced the congregation. I was next to him facing a wall, with my back to the congregation, with a stand holding the book I read from. Everything went well for a while, but at some point, I lost my place to read and when it was my turn Rabbi Tannenbaum gave me a swift kick to the back of my leg to get me started. How UNORTHODOX was that??? To this day, I never mentioned it to anybody. See, I told you that you would know more about me that nobody knew. Looking back on it, it was funny.

That night my parents threw a large Bar Mitzvah reception in downtown Paterson at the Alexander Hamilton Hotel. It was the most wonderful party and a professional shot video of the entire thing. I still have the video which was in color. See, I told you I had a great childhood. In 1958, everybody smoked cigarettes. My mother smoked Chesterfield and my father smoked up to 2 packs of Lucky

Alexander Hamilton Hotel

Strike cigarettes a day which led to lung problems later in life. So, on Bar Mitzvah night during the party, I smoked my first cigarette. I now became a "man". In the video, you can see me light and inhale my first cigarette. I smoked up to a pack a day through the years until the day I got married at the age of 26. My wife told me that if I married her, I would need to stop smoking. So, on the night of our wedding on February 26, 1972 I stopped. I was madly in love with her and would do anything. It took me over a year before I lost the craving to smoke.

How did I do it? Did I get help? NO, I did it myself. Cold turkey as they say. Did I get irritable? Yes. Did I gain weight over time? Yes. Looking back, it was rather simple in terms of stopping. I sat down and analyzed when I would smoke. It was after each meal and coffee break, first thing in the AM upon awakening, and in the PM before going to sleep. When people around me lit up, I did as well, and in the 1950's and 60's that was a lot. What I did, was after I finished eating, I would leave the table immediately. I stopped before going to bed and upon waking up. If anybody lit up a cigarette, I immediately left the room. I did not use any medicine to stop. It took a long time, with biting my nails and chewing a lot of gum. But, I did it which for me was a BIG accomplishment. I attribute our long marriage to the fact that when I am with my wife, I have no cravings, except for her and that keeps me tobacco free.

One of my mother's friends name was Margie. She ran a dance studio out of her home. My parents decided to help keep me out of mischief, I would learn to dance, specifically tap dancing and ballroom dancing. I told them there was no way that was going to happen. Then they had a great idea, my best friend Michael would also go. "No way", he told his parents. Push comes to shove, we both went and after the first day, there was no way we were going to leave. WHY, do you ask? There were 12 girls in the class and just us. WE were pubertal at the time. Just need to add 2 and 2. I learned to tap dance with tap dance shoes which I still have. Shiny black with taps on the bottom. I learned to work the bar mounted on the wall like the girls did, but could never do the splits, my anatomy prevented that. My hormones were surging so I did it all. We even had parties and played spin the bottle. Learned to dance the Tango, Fox Trot, Rumba, Cha Cha etc. Michael and I were very young but we were not stupid. Just hang a carrot in front of us and we became motivated.

One block from my grammar school # 20 there was a soda fountain, where you could get sandwiches, malteds, etc. The hamburgers were very expensive at the time, 50 cents, and 25 cents for hot dogs. That to me was very expensive. When I started driving, gasoline was only 32 cents a gallon - HIGHWAY ROBBERY!

We would spend some days, during the summer at the Hickory Hill Country Club, which was a swim club near Wayne New Jersey. They had a teenage program and one thing I really liked was riding horses. That's where I learned to ride. They would drive us down to the Circle K ranch for lessons. The first horse I rode was a very uncooperative animal. He was very pretty, chestnut brown in color and would not do anything I wanted. I even gave him sugar cubes to reward him, but even that did not help. On the very first day walking in the corral, he decided to run for the barn at a high speed. I was holding on for dear life, and then he suddenly stopped almost throwing me off his back. Despite that,

Grammar School #20

over time we began to bond. The Circle K Ranch was sold, and the large Willow Brook Mall was constructed on its site in Wayne, New Jersey.

My grandparents would winter down in Miami, Florida. One year they sent us a present. It arrived in a cardboard box with little holes in it. My father placed it on the kitchen counter and it started to move which caught us all by surprise. There was something alive in that box. We carefully opened it and a small baby alligator walked out. Unbelievable. In the early 50s you could mail alligators as gifts around the country. We placed the gator in a large deep metal container, so it could not get out and fed it salad greens. We also used to pet it. The alligator grew rapidly in size, but we still played with it. When my grandfather returned from Florida he was amazed by the rapid growth. We encouraged him to pet the little rascal and it promptly bit off the tip of his finger. We decided at that point to donate the gator to the high school biology department. Soon after that it was illegal to ship alligators out of Florida.

When I was 16, my father built a new bank in Bloomfield, New Jersey. When the construction was completed it was decided a hollow cornerstone would be added. A few selected people were asked to submit, letters, documents, pictures etc. When the bank was demolished many years later, the cornerstone - time capsule was to be opened. I was 16 and they asked me to write a letter to be added to it. Many years later they opened it and my 1962 letter was there. I included a copy of the original in this book. Three things of interest. In my letter I write about Col. John Glenn, the first American to circle the globe three times. Just a few years ago, John Glenn came to the Naples Philharmonic Hall in Naples, Florida as part of a speaker's series. I was able to ask him a question about his flight. Just totally unbelievable that I write about him at age 16 and then actually spoke to him 60 years later.

In my letter I also discuss the fear of nuclear war with the Soviet Union. At that time in April 1962, President Kennedy and Premier Nikita Khrushchev discussed ways to reach nuclear disarmament. We were extremely close to engaging Nikita Khrushchev in a nuclear war. This was a very scary time for me at the age of 16.

598 - Twentieth Avenue

Paterson 4, New Jersey

April 28, 1962

To Whom it may concern,

I am now sixteen years old. It would please me very much, if you would notify me on the finding of this letter at the above address.

I know that when this cornerstone is opened, many years will have passed, adding them to the continuing pages of history.

It is difficult to describe the times that I am now living in, for it is an age of ever changing things. I am now living in a period, which is starting to show the conquest of space. I have seen the first American pioneer to orbit the earth three times, Col. John Glenn, whom I feel you are quite familiar with. At this time, the fear of a nuclear war lingers over us as President Kennedy and Premier Khrushchev try to find a basis for world disarmament. Right now, no solution is in sight. I hope that in your age, this threat will have long ceased to exist.

In this period of history, I feel the United States, as a whole, is a very prosperous country. Through research in outer space, and our scientific efforts, I now see the coming of new instruments to lengthen the human life span. Scientists are now able to contend with many body diseases, and have just begun producing synthetic parts, to replace those of a person, who is in need of them to live.

A friend of ours, whose heart has refused to beat, is undergoing an operation to install a motor, the Pace Maker, which, by giving off electrical impulses can keep her heart beating, prolonging her life. Such are the miracles created by our scientists today. In your age, I know you will be well advanced in medical instruments and techniques.

I hope that my children and grandchildren will live in an age free and prosperity.

Sincerely,

Seth Stanley Schurman.

Time Capsule

Also, in the letter I wrote about new advances in medicine. Long before I ever considered medicine as a career. As stated, a friend of ours was having an internal pacemaker installed in her chest to keep her heart beating. The pace maker was first being used about that time. Ten years later when I was a Medical Resident, my uncle Lenny had a near fatal heart attack. I went immediately to the hospital to spend the next 24 hours with him. The hospital had three external pace makers. The first one they installed was faulty, so I had them replace it with another one, which also failed. Lucky for us the third one was the charm and he survived to live to the age of 82.

Shortly thereafter, my Aunt Esther was hospitalized with what everybody thought was terminal lung cancer. They were able to see a mass in the lung with a lot of fluid. Repeated biopsies found no evidence of cancer. When I came in to see her, they mentioned that there was nothing more that could be done. I spoke to the doctors on the case that since she was near death, that they needed to open her chest to find out what it was. Finally, they agreed. When they opened her chest, they found a large lung abscess (infection). They promptly drained it and placed her on high doses of antibiotics. She survived this near tragedy and went on to live a long life.

My father built an apartment complex with his brother in Staten Island, New York. It was built at the top of Grimes Hill, the highest point in Staten Island overlooking the Verrazano Bridge connecting Staten Island with Brooklyn, New York. The view was incredible, and you can see boat traffic traveling in and out of New York Harbor under the bridge. The apartments were rented out to college students attending Wagner College nearby. There was a long cul-de-sac at the main entrance. My father was given naming rights and he chose that it be named after me – SETH COURT. Every time I return to New York, I make a pilgrimage to Staten Island to visit my street. How neat is that! Feel free to google my street.

When I was in grammar school #20, my parents decided that I should learn to play a musical instrument. My brother learned to play the Hawaiian guitar and was pretty good at it. I decided to play the Violin, which was a total disaster. I could never position my fingers properly and could never use the

Seth Ct, Staten Island, N

ARLO RD/STRATFORD

Stratford A

Seth Ct

HOWAR
AV/SETH C

AV,

Seth Court

Seth Court Apartments

bow properly. The high-pitched screeching noises I made drove everybody away. So, I quit. My next instrument of choice was an accordion. An adult sized red and white instrument. I really wanted to play it well but was only able to master the right hand. I could never learn the left hand. In grammar school at morning assembly I would play my accordion while the other children sang along. The best thing of all was that if somebody did not like the way I played, they could not leave - a captive audience if you will. To my memory, I was never booed. I still have this accordion today and I can still play it, with one hand of course. As a side note, there was a music teacher (Mr. Butler) at the school. I got to know him quite well. He was fired on the spot when it was found out he was molesting the male students in his classes. There were three other teachers in grammar school whom I shall never forget. Miss Veith was an English teacher who also oversaw the school library. She was probably close to 80 years old and was very intelligent and the sweetest person I ever met. She had my mother, her brother, my brother, and myself as students. I helped her in the library with filing and other chores. After I left grammar school, she was my pen pal and we frequently wrote each other around holiday time, until she passed. I saved her letters. I miss her. Miss Tucker was another teacher I adored. I always looked forward to going to her class. The last teacher was Miss Bear. She was a large person and you would be punished if you spoke in her class or passed notes. Punishment consisted of placing your hands flat on the desk. She would take a wood yard ruler and hit you on the knuckles. Very painful! It never ever happened to me. I kept my mouth shut.

Do you remember ABBOTT AND COSTELLO the comedy team? Lou Costello was born and raised in Paterson, New Jersey three blocks from where I lived. I lived on East 34th Street and his family on East 33rd street. I enjoyed watching them on TV and in the movies. My grandfather and his parents were good friends. Lou was coming to town to see his parents and my grandfather was going over to see them. I begged him to take me with him, but he would not allow me to come. I was really upset! About two years later, Lou died of a heart attack.

One of their funnier routines involved Lou Costello having a tooth extracted. Abbott decided the best and easiest way to have it done and to avoid an expensive dentist visit was to tie a string to the painful tooth and tie

Lou Costello Home

the other end to a door knob. Then Abbott would quickly slam the door shut and voila the tooth would be extracted. Of course, Lou agreed to do it until it came time to slam the door shut at which time he ran after the door to avoid the pain. When I was teething, the tooth fairy would visit me after a tooth fell out and overnight miraculously a quarter would be found under my pillow. One time a tooth refused to come out easily. I wanted another quarter for candy and wanted it out. Sooo, my brother took a string and tied it to my tooth with the other end tied to the door knob. I panicked, and when he slammed the door, I also ran to avoid the pain. The tooth was ultimately left to its own schedule and fell out on its own.

There was an excellent Italian Restaurant in Paterson. It was called the Tree Tavern Restaurant. My father would take a large glass bowl with a cover and bring it to the restaurant. They would fill it up with spaghetti and meatballs and we would have a great dinner. The restaurant was located downtown next to elevated railroad tracks before entering the main downtown area. Every time a train passed, the noise was ear deafening and the entire restaurant would vibrate. The

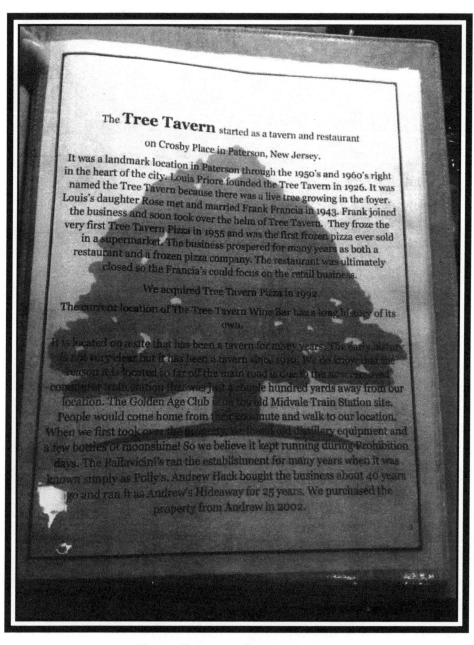

The **Tree Tavern** started as a tavern and restaurant on Crosby Place in Paterson, New Jersey.

It was a landmark location in Paterson through the 1950's and 1960's right in the heart of the city. Louis Priore founded the Tree Tavern in 1926. It was named the Tree Tavern because there was a live tree growing in the foyer. Louis's daughter Rose met and married Frank Francia in 1943. Frank joined the business and soon took over the helm of Tree Tavern. They froze the very first Tree Tavern Pizza in 1955 and was the first frozen pizza ever sold in a supermarket. The business prospered for many years as both a restaurant and a frozen pizza company. The restaurant was ultimately closed so the Francia's could focus on the retail business.

We acquired Tree Tavern Pizza in 1992.

The current location of The Tree Tavern Wine Bar has a long history of its own.

It is located on a site that has been a tavern for many years. The early history is not very clear but it has been a tavern since 1910. We do know that the reason it is located so far off the main road is due to the now removed commuter train station that was just a couple hundred yards away from our location. The Golden Age Club is on the old Midvale Train Station site. People would come home from their commute and walk to our location. When we first took over the property, we found old distillery equipment and a few bottles of moonshine! So we believe it kept running during Prohibition days. The Pallavicini's ran the establishment for many years when it was known simply as Polly's. Andrew Hack bought the business about 40 years ago and ran it as Andrew's Hideaway for 25 years. We purchased the property from Andrew in 2002.

Tree Tavern Restaurant

food from that restaurant still exists but can only be purchased in the frozen food section of the supermarket. Another restaurant was a great Jewish delicatessen. Unfortunately, the owner failed to make federal tax payments on income and it was forced to close. If you wanted the best desert you went to JAN'S ice cream parlor in Fairlawn, New Jersey. The best ice cream ever! In grammar and high school that was the place to have parties. They had what was called the kitchen sink, which was a very large bowl containing 8 or more scoops of different flavored ice cream with all the extras, including a variety of nuts, chocolate syrup, loads of whipped cream etc. Simply delicious! Jan's had multiple locations in New Jersey and New York. Today one still exists in New York and is still serving the Kitchen Sink. As a side note, a murder/suicide took place in the parking lot of that ice cream parlor. Next door to the parlor was a motel. One year, Martha Rae, the actress, was staying there performing in a night club nearby. The police were called and arrested a peeping tom looking into her room. Another great eating place was called Rutt's Hut in Clifton, New Jersey. A hang out for high schoolers which is still operating today. The Bonfire Restaurant near my home was similar to today's Diners. The food was

Kitchen Sink

Bonfire Restaurant

Rutt's Hut Restaurant

excellent back then and we ate there frequently. Today it still exists and is owned by the same family. I ate there a couple of years ago, and the food was terrible! Very disappointing. We always held our birthdays at a Howard Johnson restaurant on Route 20 in Paterson. I miss those hot dogs and especially their special hot dog bun!

Eastside Park in Paterson near my home consisted of many acres on the top of a hill overlooking East Paterson and the Passaic River. When everybody got their driver's licenses, they would on the weekends in their convertibles slowly drive around the park which was packed with high schoolers on the lookout for potential dates. A great pick up place just like in the movie American Graffiti Unfortunately, I was never successful in doing that and went home frustrated, sad to say. I was very shy, tall and very skinny only weighing 150 lbs. I also had no PERSONALITY at that time. When looking over towards East Paterson from the park, all you could see was forest for as far as the eye could see. Today all you can see is a city. In the early years they had a large fenced in area with 3 or 4 deer which you were allowed to feed and pet. One day vandals broke into the pen and cut

Howard Johnson's Restaurant

off an ear from one of them. After the episode they were removed and never seen again.

In the early part of the 20th century Paterson was the silk producing capital of the United States. Large multiple story silk mills were built around the city. These were large brick buildings encompassing full city blocks. One was located a few blocks from my home. Then, in the early 1950's, these buildings caught fire and one by one burned down. The fires were the largest I have ever seen. An arsonist was on the loose. Finally, they caught the arsonist. He was a voluntary fireman and started the fires so that he would be praised for helping put the flames out. He wanted to be a hero. How misdirected was that line of reasoning?

Let me to tell you some other interesting facts. I remember when I was just a toddler my mother placing me in a large metal vessel where she would give me sponge baths. There were no clothes washer or dryer in the early 1950s. My mother would use a serrated metal washboard in our metal sink to scrub the clothing. We also did not have a freezer. We did have a large insulated cooler. Each week the ice man would arrive in a wagon being drawn

Silk Mill

by a horse. In the back of the wagon were large pieces of ice. Using ice tongs, he would lift each slab of ice and sling it over his shoulder. He would place these large ice cubes in the insulated cooler. The ice was very heavy, and I was amazed how he was able to lift it. Then there was Newmark the dairy man delivering fresh milk to our house in glass bottles early in the morning. I never needed an alarm clock to get up in the morning. Whenever he delivered the milk, when setting it down outside our door, the bottles made a clanging noise. I think the most interesting service provider was the man who delivered coal to fire up our furnace. There were no electric heaters, just a furnace with a fire inside. We fed copious amounts of coal to it to heat the house. The method by which the coal got from the delivery truck to our basement was unique. They had a series of metal chutes that were fitted together. The highest point of the chute was at the truck, the lowest was through a window into our basement. To move the coal inside the chute they used a machine to vibrate the chute. The noise was very, very loud until all the coal was delivered. I can still relive in my mind that sound.

I must not forget the Good Humor ice cream truck which used to visit our street on

Ice Man

a weekly basis on the weekends. He would announce his arrival by ringing a loud bell. We would all run to our parents for money to buy the ice cream. My favorite was and still is their ice cream sandwich.

One day, my mother took us to New York City to see the Howdy Doodie Show with Buffalo Bob and Claribel. It was in a sound studio. On stage they had the Peanut Gallery where the children sat. There was also audience seating just off camera. My brother was chosen to be in the Peanut gallery and I sat with my mother watching the show. It was exciting for me to be there and see it all.

My brother and I would basically disagree on a lot of things and when younger we would physically have fights. One memorable time we broke a very expensive marble statue. The marble statue was that of a naked female standing on a 4 - foot marble stand with a wide base. It was a gift to my parents from a close friend named Billie who sold fur coats. This statue was in the living room at home. My parents were out the night it happened. My brother Alan was chasing me around the house and we managed to knock the statue off its pedestal. It broke into several pieces.

Alan + Seth

Marble Statue

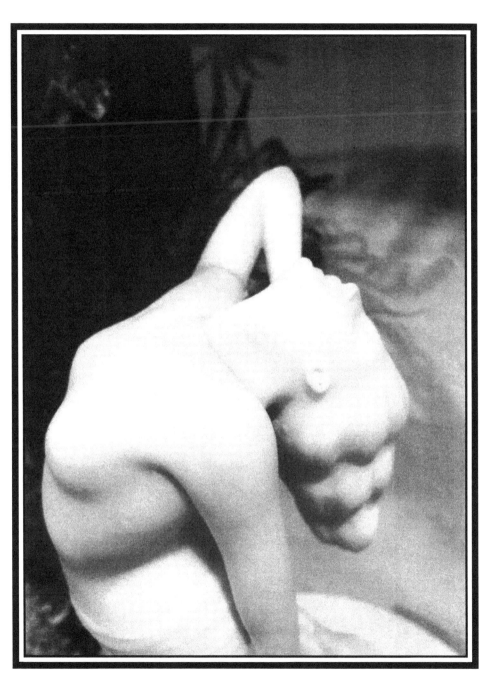

Marble Statue

We both panicked and decided we would glue the statue together and hope no one would ever notice. Of course, they did, and we owned up to what we had done. My parents were not happy. When my parents passed, I took the statue and base to my home in Fort Myers, Florida where it is displayed. In the attached picture you can see where we glued together it's arm and head.

When I was nine years old, I saved $ 40.00 from my allowance to purchase the first transistor AM radio. It was manufactured by the Regency Company. There was a jewelry shop one block from my home. I remember walking with my father to the shop to buy that radio. It was the first monetary purchase of my life and it is clearly imbedded in my mind. About 2 years ago I found it and they no longer make the square batteries to power it. I went to the Batteries Plus Store and the technician was able to create a battery back that came within 2 volts of the original battery. We turned it on and the radio turned on and played as it did 63 years ago. We were all excited about getting it to work again. Sounds as good as the day I brought it! Another miracle!

Regency Transistor Radio

My first box camera was the Brownie Hawkeye Camera Flash Model, which my father brought for me in the early 1950s. I used it for the first time when we visited Niagara Falls. My father took pictures of me carrying that camera. I still have it and it also sits on my desk, now 65 years later, with the original pop out flash bulbs. I wish I could still buy the film for it.

My mother was a terrible cook. My father would only eat food that was well done. At 5 PM daily we would all eat dinner together. My brother and I ate very little which would explain how thin I was. Lucky for us there was a large potted plant next to the table. At breakfast we were required to have orange juice. I did not like orange juice and when my mother was facing in a different direction, I poured the juice into the potted plant. That was my savior and she never caught on.

I must not forget the large fig and cherry trees we grew. My father planted one of the first fig trees in the state of New Jersey. Each year, it produced hundreds of delicious figs. More than enough to gift teachers, friends, and relatives. For 15 years we enjoyed the most delicious figs you would ever eat. One

Brownie Hawkeye Camera

would ask, how does such a tree survive the brutal winters and frequent snow storms that were common in the fifties and sixties? At the end of each season in late fall, the tree would shed its large fig leaves. We would tie a rope around the tree and stuff the fallen leaves inside the limbs. Next, the tree was securely wrapped in heavy canvas. As spring approached, the tree sprung back to life and gifted us with more figs.

My father's parents lived on Van Buren street in Passaic, New Jersey. In the back of the house, they planted a cherry tree. Each year it grew in size and we were treated to large red cherries, hundreds of them. We would collect them either with a ladder, or by opening a second story window to reach them. Those were the most delicious cherries I ever ate! That tree survived every winter without any special treatment. I miss the taste of those juicy red cherries.

In another vivid memory, I was sitting at the dining table. My mother was near the sink and was eating a piece of chicken, when a bone lodged in her throat and she could not breath. My brother at that time was interested in medicine as early as high school.

He quickly ran to her and using the Heimlich maneuver several times was able to dislodge the bone and saved her life. Had he not been there, she would have died. I did not have a clue what to do.

My mother was a talented figure skater when she was young and competitively skated, winning several awards.

As a child, my mother used to sing to me. Her favorite song was "Because of You", recorded by Tony Bennett in 1951. This was his first hit. To this day I remember her singing it to me. Point of interest - Tony Bennett continues to visit Fort Myers and sing as well.

Thanksgiving was a special time of year. We would have a huge feast with relatives and friends. My father would cook the turkey and it was delicious. On one occasion when I was very young, he invited me to go with him to select the best turkey. One of his friends operated a large poultry farm. When we arrived, I was impressed with the large-facility. My father picked out one of the turkeys. Next, I experienced one of the ugliest things I ever saw. To prepare the turkey, they first had to kill it. They would take the turkey and insert it head first into a machine that decapitated it. The bird was screaming to the very end. It was terrible. Needless to say, I never ever went back with him to get a turkey. I ATE NO TURKEY THAT YEAR!

Point of historical interest - during prohibition alcohol was being boot legged. This was done in many ways. Waxy Gordon developed a unique way to distribute the booze to the various speakeasies. He connected the distillery to them using garden hoses using the sewer system to avoid detection. The infamous city where that occurred was Paterson, New Jersey.

Not to be forgotten, the issue of global warming which everyone has been focused on. While growing up in New Jersey in the 1950's the winters were severe. We would have major snowstorms every few weeks dumping several feet of snow. It was difficult shoveling it all. The public schools were frequently closed because of snow days and we had to make them all up later in the season. Today New Jersey only gets light snow most of the time. This can only be explained by global warming.

My fondest memory was opening my window in the middle of the night watching the snow gently fall around the street light. It was so quiet you could actually hear it falling to the ground. I was mesmerized watching and listening to it.

My brother and I were required to wear a tie and jacket when we went out for dinner in the 1950 and 1960s. Everybody used to do that. Now, when you go out to the fanciest restaurants, casual wear is the norm. Casual to the degree that when you visit a top-rated steak house for example, people wear shorts, or T shirts or jeans.

CHAPTER 7
High School and College

I attended Eastside High School in Paterson, New Jersey from January 1959 to January 1963. School entrance was in 6-month intervals. I enjoyed math and sciences but didn't really care for English courses. We were required to take a foreign language course, and I chose French. Why did I choose French? I have no idea - I hated every bit of it! The whole class was conducted in French, and I had no clue what was going on. Whenever I entered the class I would sit in the back of the room and slump in my chair, so the teacher would not see me. Whenever she did, I was unable to converse with her. She was one smart woman. She had all our names on cue cards and she would call on us one by one. There was no escaping her. I remember how to count in French and to this day can recite a sentence (la plume de ma tante sur la table). It means my aunt's pen is on the table. I visited France

Eastside High School

in later years and that sentence did not help me one bit. I begged the teacher not to fail me and out of the goodness of her heart gave me a D, which was my lowest grade in high school.

One semester I had an exchange teacher from Hawaii who was wonderful. The one thing she taught me that I will never forget is the Hawaiian word for Merry Christmas (Mele Kalikimaka).

In high school I had an interest in acting and joined the Drama Club which was directed by Miss George. One memorable play we did was *Old Towne* written by Gene Wilder. I was cast as the town drunk. It was a lot of fun, never knowing who would mess up their lines. Everyone loved that play.

It was in high school that I became infatuated with a wonderful girl named J.S. I will not embarrass her by revealing her real name. She was my first love interest. One day I received a phone call at home from a girl, whose voice I did not recognize. We talked for a few days, but she refused to reveal to me who she was. She had a sultry sexy voice and I was entranced by this mysterious caller. Then one day a mutual friend of hers approached me and invited me to a house party. It was common in those days to have house parties with parents as chaperones. It was there that she revealed herself to me and we began dating. Her father was a drug representative for a large pharmaceutical company. As a gift he gave me a paper weight consisting of a doctor treating a patient, long before I chose medicine as a career. She had the nicest parents. To make a long story short we parted ways. As recently as a year ago through an online site we were able to reconnect with each other exchanging letters after a lapse of fifty years.

There were other girlfriends during my high school years. They included Sandy Rosen, Esther Rifkin, Jane Levin, and all of them are online to this day. One sad note - Barry Glick was also a friend and when the World Trade Center was attacked in 2011, he was in one of the towers and perished. I have communicated with his wife since that tragedy.

Another side note. Many years after I left High School a movie was produced called *Lean on Me* with Morgan Freeman. It was about the worst High School in New Jersey, specifically Eastside High my alma mater. When I attended the school, it was not an upper crust school but it produced a lot of successful professional people. After I left, it became a serious inner - city school with drugs and crime running rampant. The movie dealt with Joe Clark the Principal who fought to bring up the academic level and rid the school of all the thugs and dope addicts and eliminate the crime. He would carry a baseball bat and bull horn and roamed the halls. Over time the high school turned around. The movie was about him and my alma mater and was filmed entirely on location at the school. Every time I see that film, I revisit my high school.

I also had a close encounter with someone sleep walking. One summer, I painted apartments in my father's development (the same development I tripped and fell into wet cement). I lived with my father's long - term carpenter Frank and his family in one of the units. The bedrooms were on the second floor and I shared a bedroom with his son Bobbie who was around 14 years old at that time. There was a long staircase leading downstairs. One night at around 2 AM, Bobbie began talking in his sleep. All of a sudden, he got out of bed and in total darkness ran down the flight of stairs and left the apartment. We ran after him and walked him back to the apartment without fully awakening him. I never experienced this before or after. How he could run down a flight of stairs and do what he did, I cannot explain. To this day, I think about that night.

While I was in high school, John F. Kennedy and Richard M. Nixon were campaigning for the U.S. presidency. They both visited Paterson, holding rallies on the steps of City Hall. My high school gave us the day off to see them. I was able to get within a couple of feet of John Kennedy but was unable to shake his hand. However, when Nixon came, I was able to shake his hand. Very exciting seeing them both up close!

I attended Bloomfield College in Bloomfield, New Jersey with a major in Chemistry. The department chairman was Thomas A. Wilson PhD. He was a brilliant chemist and worked on the Manhattan Project which developed the Atomic Bomb.

One of the professors was a Psychologist. She used to administer all sorts of tests to me. To this day, I do not remember what she found. Could I have failed them miserably? I don't know, but I enjoyed taking them. One thing she did whenever I visited her was to break open and eat raw eggs. Why, I do not know, but I saw her do it on numerous occasions. Funny the things you remember.

Another professor I studied under was a Philosopher. The way he spoke and his mannerisms were out of a movie. We were instructed to write a philosophical paper about death. My paper concluded that when you die, time stops. I aced the course. The professor stated that it was one of the best papers he read.

My father would always say that the time of our death is written in a book. It is preordained. I would ask him, if a plane crashed with 200 people on board and they all died, did they all have the same date?

The most frightening experience and the closest I ever came to dying occurred when I was driving my Bonneville Pontiac home from Bloomfield College on the Garden State Parkway. For me, this was a life changing event. I was driving home in a terrible thunder and lightning storm in the left lane. The water was puddling on the road and I lost control of my car. The median was full of trees and a cement overpass was rapidly approaching. My car skidded and went into the median at 60 miles per hour heading directly into the cement overpass. I took the steering wheel and quickly turned as far to the left as possible. My car went into several spins thankfully avoiding the trees and eventually stopped with the front of the car at the edge of the road perpendicular to the roadway, as cars sped by within a couple of feet. Thank G-D I did not hit the concrete wall or trees and was not back on the roadway where cars would impact me. I sat there in total shock, my hands glued to the steering wheel and my whole body shaking. My car could have hit a tree, the concrete overpass, or ended up back on the roadway and struck by cars speeding by. It took me a while to regain my composure, and eventually proceed home. My personality completely changed after that experience. I was very shy and introverted prior to this episode. After it happened, I became noticeably extroverted and came out of my shell. I could not believe I survived! Everyone around me saw the difference in my personality literally overnight. To this day whenever I drive on a highway during storms, I am always cognizant of the puddling of water on the roadway and drive slowly. I remember that night as if it occurred yesterday.

When my paternal grandmother passed away, she was interred at a nearby cemetery. The gravesite ceremony took place at the same time services were conducted for Milton Berle's mother a few steps away. I will never forget seeing him at the gravesite.

I majored in Chemistry in college. During my junior year, Schering pharmaceutical company donated an obsolete drug development complex to our school. I, with a few of my classmates, were chosen to move our chemistry laboratory into this facility. One day one of my fellow students broke a 5-gallon jug of hydrochloric acid down the hall from where I was working. Unknown to me the ventilation system carried the fumes towards me. As I walked to help them contain the spill, I was overcome by the fumes and developed difficulty breathing and a burning sensation in my chest. I lost consciousness as they dragged me to an open window to get fresh air. Obviously, I survived, but my lung function testing has always been abnormal.

I will never forget where I was on the day of John F. Kennedy's assassination. I was visiting my brother who was in the chemistry lab at Bloomfield College in Bloomfield, New Jersey. There was a small television in the lab when the news was released. I was in total shock and disbelief and cried. It was like the whole world had stopped. We were listening to Walter Cronkite deliver the news.

The next morning, Lee Harvey Oswald, the accused murderer was to be transferred to another jail facility. I got up early the next morning to watch the transfer live on TV. I actually witnessed the first murder ever committed on live TV. That broadcast will live with me forever. The officer who was escorting Oswald, the man with the large white hat, recently passed away at the age of 99.

As another point of interest. My high school graduation took place in January, 1963. I entered college in February, 1963 and graduated in June of 1966. I completed college in three and a half years. In order to do that, I was required to complete all the prerequisites required for either a PhD in chemistry or for the medical field. The three summers were spent taking such courses as organic chemistry, physics, and calculus. These were very intense courses taken during the summer on a short time table. This was the main reason that I was the youngest freshman in medical school at the age of twenty. All of this was exhausting but well worth it.

CHAPTER 8
Medical School

How did I become a physician? Why did I become a physician? The answer to both these questions will surprise you. Although my brother was a physician, I had no burning desire to become one. My undergraduate degree was a B.A. in chemistry. For some reason I became interested in radiation chemistry. To that end I applied to Ohio State University in Columbus, Ohio, and received a Teaching Assistant grant in the field of Radiation Chemistry. As a side note, I flew out for an interview at the university. At that time, they had a large campus with thousands of students. I will never forget standing in the center of the campus in a very large open area. There was nobody to be seen. Then, a bell went off which signaled a change in classes and suddenly, thousands of students poured out of the buildings to change classes. That sight I will never forget!

My father accompanied me to Ohio. He had an intense fear of flying. As the plane was taking off, he grasped both arm rests with such force that his knuckles turned white. I still remember that.

My father was a strong believer in education. My brother was admitted to the Chicago Medical School. He had always wanted to become a physician. After our trip to Ohio, and upon my acceptance into their program, he sat me down and told me that I should consider going to medical school. He told me that I would always be an employee and would not be in control of my future. I told him that I was not really interested in doing that, but after a long discussion, I agreed to send an application to only one medical school, specifically the one my brother was in. If by some outside chance I would be accepted I would give it a try. There were 16 applicants for the seat that I applied for, and I was accepted. Before I was accepted, I went to Chicago for an interview. The weather there is very changeable. The day I left their temperature was in the 50s. I took a lined raincoat as my only jacket. The next day in Chicago, the temperature dropped to subzero, and stayed there for the few days I was there. Quite an introduction to Chicago weather! As a side note - when I arrived in Chicago while moving in, the temperature was 104 degrees.

I notified Ohio State University that I was accepted to Medical School and decided to enter the field of medicine. They sent me a wonderful letter congratulating me on my acceptance and wishing me success. They also mentioned that if I ever decided medicine was not my true calling, they would leave an opening for me to return and pursue radiation chemistry.

The summer prior to moving to Chicago, I volunteered at the Barnhart Memorial Hospital in Paterson. My duties included stocking all the medical units and I would also help transport the recently deceased patients to the basement to a refrigerated storage area just like in the movies. That was my first encounter with a dead body. The one thing I cannot forget was the name tag attached to the big toe of the deceased.

The winds in Chicago were unbelievable and walking was difficult at times. The first year I would walk about five long blocks to get on a train which dropped me off in front of my medical school. There were days I thought I could not make it. The wind almost blew me off my feet. Chicago has always been known as the windy city. Truth in fact, it received that designation to describe the blustery politicians that were there. Many people who were born and raised there thought it was because of the wind.

I shared an apartment with my brother on Harvard Street in Forest Park, Illinois, a western suburb of Chicago. It was a garden style apartment on the first floor with a large picture window in front. Our next door neighbors were Emily and George Ostrowski with their son Bobby. They became a second family, inviting me over for many meals and to socialize. They offered me a lot of support and I could never thank them enough. Bobby and I would go out to an occasional movie as well.

One of our neighbors had a very large St. Bernard dog that he used to walk past our building. It must have weighed 400 pounds and was the largest dog I ever saw. It was a very friendly dog. One day while I was outside he walked past me, and decided to put his paws on me and knocked me off my feet. I will never forget that.

Nearby was a White Castle Hamburger restaurant where I loved to eat their small square hamburgers. Another restaurant of note was an expensive continental restaurant nearby. My brother and I would eat there once a week. The steaks were excellent. One very curious thing was when we would eat there the parking lot was always full with very few diners inside even at peak dining hour. Then one day the restaurant was raided and shut down. Why? Because they operated a gambling hall in the back room.

Medical School for me did not come easy. The first two years were basic science studies, the last two were introduction to clinical medicine, the part I loved the most. The

White Castle Hamburgers

White Castle Square Burger

very first day we had to read two chapters of a book we were using. We were behind from day one. When we entered class on the first day, we were presented with a test that we needed to complete. The instructor told us to read it over in its entirety before starting to answer the questions. I read it over and at the very end it stated that the test should not be taken. Most of the students started answering the questions. An important lesson learned! I spent hours and hours of didactics sitting on hardwood seats in a large amphitheater in the original school building on South Wolcott Avenue. Then I went home to study for hours. I only had six hours of sleep a night and very few breaks. It was so difficult! Most of my classmates took medicine to keep them awake. I never did. I decided that at twelve midnight I would stop studying and go to sleep. What would be would be. We would have our names and grades posted on a bulletin board in the lobby of the school for everyone to see. It was like hanging out dirty laundry. It was demeaning but I suppose motivated us to study harder. I was mostly in the middle of my class which consisted of 80 male and 1 female student. Pop quizzes were given almost every day and the stress was overwhelming. Then one day on one of the tests I scored top in my class, but because so many failed it the teacher threw out all the grades. I was very angry. I compare my experience from the first two years to being brainwashed.

One block from the school was a restaurant called the Greeks. Talk about a greasy spoon. Medical students, transients, all sorts of beggars found that restaurant. Of all the things on the menu they had a Thurenger Francheze. It consisted of a fat hot dog, split and filled with American cheese then wrapped in bacon on a hot dog bun. Greasy as heck but the most delicious hot dog I ever had. I ate there for lunch and had the same dog daily while I watched winos drinking wine out of bottles hidden in paper bags.

The first year involved human anatomy with dissection of the human body. I entered medical school before my 21st birthday. I was the youngest student in my class. My parents had to sign a special authorization form before I was allowed in the dissection lab. Four students were assigned to one body throughout. The bodies were preserved in formaldehyde. Day after day, the odor was so strong it permeated our lab coats (that odor will never be forgotten). No matter how many times I laundered my whites, the odor remained.

The Greeks

Across the street from the front entrance of the hospital is a one-story building called "University Inn Restaurant" better known as the "Greeks". All interns and residents have frequented the "Greeks" and it played a significant part of their social life.

The Greeks Restaurant

One semester we had Autopsy class which was held in Hektoen Institute across from Cook County Hospital. Once a week we would observe autopsies and based upon the results would postulate what medical problems the deceased had and to determine step wise the cause of death. Forensics are very interesting. The most memorable autopsy was on a middle - aged man. During the autopsy when they opened his abdomen the found a large worm later identified as Schistosomiasis which caused his untimely death. Later it was found that he had been out of the country and swam in fresh water rivers loaded with this parasite.

After surviving the first two years we were introduced to clinical medicine. Now things got interesting. The laying on of hands to diagnose and treat real patients. Eli Lilly, a pharmaceutical company presented each of us with a black doctor's bag with our names engraved in gold on it. Inside was a stethoscope, tuning fork, reflex hammer, and a few other things. Each semester we rotated thru different specialties where interns and residents would take us on rounds, hold conferences with us along with attending physicians, and then allow us to examine live patients. We learned how to take histories and conduct full physical examinations.

Most of our rotations were at Cook County Hospital across from our medical school. I did my obstetrics rotation there. I also delivered 16 babies by myself with virtually no supervision after the second delivery. Not bad for a 22 - year old. Cook County Hospital was originally a 3,000 - bed institution for the indigent patients of Cook County. The obstetric ward consisted of two laboring areas on each end with maybe 12 beds. There were about 6 birthing rooms separating both areas. When women went into labor, they were placed in the labor rooms. There were days you would enter the labor rooms and it would be relatively quiet. When they brought in a screamer, all the other woman would start to scream. When time came for transfer into the birthing room it was important that the women empty their bladders. One trick that was used would be to go to the sink and turn on the water. The flow of water into the sink resulted in urination by the patient. If this failed the patient was catheterized. When I started my rotation, there was one resident and one intern in the unit. They taught me how to deliver a baby with an episiotomy incision and how to sew

Cook County Hospital

up the cut with catgut. Then when more than two patients were to deliver, I was the only one besides a nurse, delivering the patient. What a messy experience, but I loved it. I will never forget I was delivering a woman who was on her 8th child. When I was ready for her to push, the baby flew out of her womb and hit me in the stomach. I fumbled but was able to catch the baby before it hit the floor. On another occasion, after a woman delivered her baby, she asked me if it was black or white.

On one occasion a female was being treated for pelvic inflammatory disease. When she was examined, she had a bifurcate uterus, cervix and vagina meaning she had two of each. Very rare. She was aware of it and when she had relations either vagina would be used.

Another interesting patient we saw had transposition of the great vessels. In other words, the vessels and heart were on the opposite side of the body. When examining his heart, you could not hear any heart sounds on the left side, but they could be clearly heard on the right side. A very rare condition.

On another occasion there was a small outbreak of Diphtheria, and we visited a children's hospital to examine the children. On examination you could see lesions or membranes in the throat. A very serious infection which results in death if not caught early.

We also visited a large mental hospital. Easy to flash back to the film *One Flew Over the Cuckoo's Nest* starring Jack Nicholson, although that film was released later. It was an eye-opening experience and I had nightmares after that visit.

On my Psychiatry rotation we would spend 45 minutes alone with a patient in a room and were instructed on how to question them. The rooms consisted of a desk and 2 chairs on opposite sides of it. We were instructed to always take the seat closest to the door for a quick exit if the patient became violent. On interviewing the patient, we would ask questions. For example, "how do you feel about that?" or "tell me what is upsetting you?" These were leading questions to allow the patients to vent their emotions. I was never qualified to suggest solutions. I was only 22 years old. It was felt that if we let them talk out their problems, they would feel better upon leaving. One patient I saw on a weekly basis was a crier. From the minute we sat down all she would do is cry. Nothing I said made her feel better. I never had to make a fast exit from that room!

On my Internal Medicine rotation, I experienced the funniest moment of my career. I would see new patients and do history and physicals on them. When I was done, I would go into the doctor's office where I would present the case to a Resident and Intern. One woman I evaluated must have weighed easily 350 pounds which was morbidly obese. I did the history and then did the physical. Her breasts were very large and to listen to her heart I had to lift her left breast with one hand and place my stethoscope under her breast with the other. After I finished, I pulled my stethoscope out from under the breast. I completed my exam and then proceeded to the Doctor's office to present the case. When I walked in both the Resident and Intern began to laugh hysterically and pointed to my stethoscope which was missing the metal bell at the end of it. When I pulled the stethoscope out from under her breast, the bell came off the end. I was totally embarrassed. I went back into her room and told her what happened. I then lifted the breast and retrieved the missing part.

On my cardiology rotation we studied the heart and circulatory system. One night they admitted a 27-year-old male suffering a heart attack in evolution. He continued to have severe chest pain as more and more heart muscle was destroyed. There was nothing we could do and after a couple of hours he died in front of us. He had a terrible family history of high cholesterol. His was measured at 2000 where normal is considered under 200. His brother, two years older than him, also died very young with high cholesterol. At that time, we had no medicines available to lower it.

The Chicago Medical School was built about the turn of the century on Wolcott Avenue. Most of our classes were taken in a large amphitheater, a very small version of today's Hollywood Bowl. The lecturer was at a podium at the bottom and we sat in a half circle configuration with each row of seats oriented higher and higher. It was surreal and reminded me of some of the old horror movies. After we completed our second year of classes and went on a short break, the roof of that class room totally caved in. If anyone had been inside it, they would have perished.

The weather in Chicago was abysmal ranging from boiling hot to frigid cold. I was in the worst snowstorm that Chicago ever experienced in 1969. The weather forecasters predicted the evening that the snow started that we should expect between one and three inches. I went to bed and when I awoke the next morning, I was unable to see out my apartment window. I thought it was wind driven snow and nothing more. When I opened my front door, I encountered a solid wall of snow. Chicago was hit with a 27" snow fall overnight. A city record with windblown drifts up to six feet high. Using a shovel, I was able to exit my apartment and that was as far as I got. The city was buried and shut down for about five days. It took us two days to clear the parking lot in our apartment complex. We could not drive anywhere because the roads were clogged with snow. It was the first time in history that my medical school was shut down for several days. The city had nowhere to put the snow as they started plowing. It was decided they would collect the snow in dump trucks and dump it into Lake Michigan. An arduous process!

Another weather dilemma were the ice storms which coated the ground with ice.

1969 Snowstorm

This included black ice which you could not see. I was driving a Simca which was a small four door car. As a side note, the gas mileage was amazing, almost 35 miles to the gallon, and this was way back in 1968. The car was tiny and I had to fold myself like an accordion to get into it. It was stick shift which I had to learn as well. The car was so small I felt like a circus clown. It was so small I could have taken out the front seat and driven it from the rear one. The car only had a useful life of a few years and was literally disposable, but it did for me what it had to do.

In the suburbs of Chicago, there was literally no drainage of water from the road surface. The rains in Chicago are the worst I ever experienced. They occurred frequently and would cause white outs. I was barely able to see the hood on my car. All the cars would stop almost completely until the rains let up. You would be on the expressway, the rain would start, and the cars would totally stop. The roads were built with the road surface at its highest point in the center and then tapering steeply towards the curb on each side. My first experience with black ice occurred in the suburbs. One day, there was a terrible ice storm. I decided to drive to my school on city streets and not the expressway. As I was driving near the center of the road, my car began sliding sideways towards the curb. I felt totally helpless and unable to control it. Luckily no other cars were nearby. Before I began sliding the road surface appeared to be clear of ice, but I was wrong. It was black ice which was a rude awakening.

Another severe weather episode occurred the year before. The worst tornado outbreak in Chicago history. Fifty - five people were killed during that storm. It started south of my apartment wiping out a shopping complex, skipped over my apartment, and killed many more just north of my location. I was outside during the storm and noticed that the storm clouds were bobbing up and down as they rapidly moved. I did not have video at that time and could not record it. I have never in my life seen clouds do what they did. On another occasion, a tornado entered the city of Chicago from the western suburbs and this was well documented. It was a rare event for the downtown area.

When visiting Dr. Demas, a Pulmonary Specialist on the 6th floor of Mount Sinai Hospital in Chicago, the building began to shake. All the glass doors on the bookcases began rattling. It lasted a few minutes and then subsided. We thought the building was going to collapse. Later it was explained that a 5.3 earthquake occurred in the northeast part of Iowa. Anyone in Chicago above the 4th floor of any building felt that quake.

I lived in Chicago when Richard Speck murdered seven student nurses a few miles away from where I lived.

I also lived in Chicago during the 1968 Democratic National Convention. Rioting was the worst the city ever experienced. I lived a few miles west of downtown. The medical center was near the downtown area along the Eisenhower Expressway. The rioters set fires for miles on each side of the expressway. The Governor called out the National Guard. It was surreal driving from my apartment to the Medical School. All the buildings on both sides of the expressway were in flames. The medical center was occupied by armed troops and tanks. They had to secure the area because of sniper attacks. It was like a war zone.

One memorable place I used to visit on weekends was OLD TOWN. Located on Wells

Avenue and State street this consisted of a party area with bars, loud music and the best steaks you could eat. It resembled New Orleans. The streets would close, and everybody came to party. Over the years this area disappeared. There are only small historic street signs designating where it used to be. What a big loss for everybody.

On one occasion my current girlfriend and I drove to Milwaukee, Wisconsin about a two-hour drive for a day trip. At that time the city was known as the beer capital of the world. It was a shocking introduction to the city. We drove into the city from the west. We encountered a bridge over a deep canyon and were instantly downtown. I was not prepared for what I encountered. The strong odor of beer permeated the entire city. You could literally get drunk just inhaling it. Totally unexpected. We ate at a wonderful German Restaurant while there, the name escapes me. We also visited Mitchell park which contained the three domes. They are three large glass domes each representing geographic areas, for example one contained a desert environment, another a tropical rain forest, and the third would change seasonally. They are still there today, and I highly recommend it. Of course, the Wisconsin cheese was

Mitchell Park Domes

Three Domes

the best. We learned that it is illegal to import cheese into the state.

My apartment in Forest Park was next to Cicero where Al Capone had residence during the mob years. My father visited some friends in the area. They operated a restaurant and would deliver food to Al and his gang. My father went with them and met Al.

I was dating another girl and she took me to a house party. When first entering the home, there was a white cloud of smoke filling it. It had a very sweet smell, and despite the fact I never smoked marijuana I knew what it was immediately, and I left. I knew if I stayed and it was raided, and I was found there, my medical career would be over.

One unforgettable incident happened when I was returning home from the hospital around 1 AM. To understand the situation better, allow me to describe what Chicago was like in 1967. The mayor of Chicago was Richard Daley. He ran a very tight ship in a city that was riddled with crime. His police force consisted of very large policemen, which I would describe as the size of refrigerators. Cook County Hospital and the west side of Chicago were nasty neighborhoods especially at night. I left the hospital in my small Simca automobile and was on an access road to gain entry to the Eisenhower Expressway. I was wearing my whites which were our work clothes. The streets around me were devoid of cars. Suddenly, a police car with lights flashing and siren running pulled me over. Before I knew it, a refrigerator sized police officer ran up to my window holding a pistol, aimed at ME. It took a few minutes to defuse the situation explain I was a medical student returning home from the hospital. He scared the crap out of me! I was driving over the speed limit but not by very much. His police were ultra- proactive.

Mayor Daley died while still in office when I was in Chicago. He had an appointment to see his physician for a checkup because he had a history of heart disease. He was placed in an exam room to wait for the doctor and had a fatal heart attack. They were unable to resuscitate him. An end of an era for Chicago politics.

One of my friends at school was from West Falmouth, Massachusetts. He decided to cook a lobster in his apartment. His parents sent a live large lobster from home. It was dark grey green in coloration. He purchased a very large pot with a heavy metal lid to cook it. I had no idea what was to come next. It was ugly as I watched the process. He filled the pot with water, adding salt and other seasonings. In my mind I could not believe what happened next. This live lobster was placed into the pot and my friend firmly held the lid on tightly to prevent its escape. The lobster began screaming and squealing and fought to get out. Kicking the pot violently. It turned my stomach watching this process. When the cooking was complete and the lobster was removed, its shell color turned bright red. The whole process shocked me and to this day I do not remember if I ever ate from it. As a side note, I was the Best Man at his wedding in West Falmouth, Massachusetts.

When I was in my senior year of medical-school we were allowed to shadow a family practitioner, and follow him full time in examining and treating real time patients. It was a wonderful experience! The physician I selected practiced in Hinsdale, Illinois about a 45-minute drive from Chicago. I would drive daily to meet him. It was a beautiful drive through cornfields. The town was something out of a Norman Rockwell painting. It was so laid back and was one of the most beautiful cities I ever visited. Today it is a modernized bustling city. Its charm has been lost, sad to say. It deserves honorable mention in my book.

My brother was two years ahead of me in medical school. On one occasion I visited him while he was on his Emergency Room rotation. One of the cardinal rules in medical training is that you see a procedure done once and you are expected to do the next one. On this fateful day, a patient came in with a dislocated shoulder. My brother was alone as other physicians were occupied elsewhere. He decided to repair the dislocated shoulder himself without seeing it done previously. He went into the physician's office, and located an orthopedic textbook and quickly studied the step by step procedure to re-establish the shoulder. He went to the patient, tried it and failed. He returned to the book several times, in and out, and finally corrected the problem. The patient was not happy with the time it took, nor the pain involved.

Another very disturbing scene involved a patient brought int the Emergency Room, hemorrhaging from the esophagus. He was a known alcoholic with advanced liver disease. The inserted a long tube into his esophagus and it was inflated to stop the bleeding. The patient was in extreme distress and awake. Despite multiple blood transfusions, they were unable to stop the bleeding and I watched as the patient died. This really upset me and was a traumatic experience.

All of these experiences contributed to not only teach you how to diagnose and treat a patient, but to also harden you to the worst things you would encounter in the future. You learn to dissociate your emotions and focus on getting positive results. It is very difficult.

I must not forget the cars that transported me all those years. As mentioned previously, I began driving in Liberty, New York at the age of 15. That car was a 1953 pale green Cadillac and I took my driving test in that car. It was built like a Sherman Tank and the gas mileage was terrible. On the front and back bumper there were two large chrome "bullets" to protect the car in case of an accident. While driving my grandparents to the train station to catch a train for Florida, we were stopped at a light and we were rear ended. It was quite a jolt! It was surprising to find that our car had barely a scratch, while the other car that hit us was badly damaged.

When commuting to college, my parents bought me a 1966 Bonneville Pontiac con- vertible. It was white with a burgundy red interior and retractable roof. The car was gorgeous. It was also a gas guzzler.

When attending Medical School in Chicago, my parents brought me a Simca which is man- ufactured in France. The car was a four - door sedan about the size of a small Volkswagen. It was really tiny and being 6'4" tall I had to fold myself like an accordion to get into it. Alas, I joke about it, but it was great on dates, and had great gas mileage. This was in 1967.

After I got married, we inherited my father- in-law's car. My wife had her own car. We ran both of them up to 85,000 miles.

Our first car purchased was a Dodge Dart Sports car. We both loved that car. We put probably 80,000 miles on that car and then traded it in for a Cadillac. We went to the dealership where the car was inspected and we negotiated a deal. A couple of days later

Simca Automobile

when they started the car, the engine exploded and all the parts fell to the ground. Very funny, because the last time we started it, it ran fine. The salesman was not laughing. Luckily, we got a good allowance on trade in.

From the time I started flying, I experienced four incidents, three of which were life threatening. The first occurred my fourth year in college. I decided to take a trip to Club Med on the Island of Martinique for a one-week vacation. The trip there was uneventful. The return trip was hair raising. We were flying along the New Jersey coast in-route to Newark Airport. We were all enjoying a full breakfast when suddenly we got into severe turbulence which was violent. I thought the plane would break in half. We were instructed to take all our food trays and throw them into the aisle. The most violent experience I ever had on a plane, and it lasted a very long time. People were screaming and crying. After we landed safely, we all had to walk over the food and trays and drinks that were thrown in the aisle. A very scary incident!

The first time I flew alone was when I went to be interviewed for Medical School. At the airport my father engaged an army soldier who was returning home on leave. He knew I was afraid and arranged to have the soldier sit next to me to calm my fears. This soldier was a paratrooper, and all the way to Chicago he discussed jumping out of airplanes. THAT did not calm me down one bit!

On another trip to Chicago, I was booked on to the same flight, number, day and time one week after the same plane exploded and crashed into Lake Michigan with no survivors. I was not happy!

On another flight to Chicago we were over Lake Michigan in a very heavy fog. All of a sudden, we heard over the sound system the pilot yelling to another plane to get off our wing. As the fog cleared, we could see the other plane, close enough to see the passenger's eyes. A very close call. Both planes separated and both planes landed safely. I will never be a fan of flying.

CHAPTER 9
Residency and Fellowship

After completing medical school, I did a Medical Internship and first year Medical Residency at Maimonides Medical Center and a second year Medical Residency at Brookdale Hospital. I then entered a two - year Allergy Fellowship program at Long Island College Hospital. All my training was completed in Brooklyn, New York.

I rented a second floor flat in a two - story private home about three blocks from Maimonides. It was rent controlled which made it affordable for the five years I lived there. Mr. and Mrs. Kostenbader, an older German couple were the owners and occupied the first floor and part of the second floor. She was a wonderful cook and would offer me food on occasion. We asked around and learned from the hospital about this apartment. It was occupied by an Orthopedic Resident and his wife. He was finishing his training and they were moving. Their name was Rockfeld. I met both of them and it was agreed I would be the next tenant.

The Rockfeld's were relocating to, of all places, Naples, Florida where he would practice Orthopedics. A couple of years into my training I learned that on one fateful day he rented a boat with his wife, who was pregnant, to venture into the Gulf of Mexico. The owner of the boat rental company told them that a storm was brewing and recommended they don't take the boat out. Despite the warnings, they went out with the boat and he was the only one who came back. She was lost at sea. Her parents were very wealthy and had placed over a million dollars into her bank account and he was to come into a very rich inheritance. They had two young children who were placed into the custody of her parents. He wanted custody but they refused. It was believed that he deliberately took her out into the storm to murder her but he was never charged with murder and her body was never recovered. After a prolonged legal battle, it was decided Doctor Rockfeld would receive his inheritance, but the children were to be raised by her parents. He left Naples, and a few years ago, he passed away.

Internship and Residency training were very intense with sleep deprivation from being on call every third night. It would always begin early in the morning and continue all day, all night, and the entire next day before you would literally crash. Almost 36 hours each time with very little sleep. Every third weekend you would be on call from Friday early morning until Monday evening, with very little sleep. This was years before they determined too many medical errors occurred because of it, and they drastically reduced work hours. Add on all the conferences, medical rounds, and other required activities, it was almost near impossible to survive. It was all a form of brain washing.

Medical conferences were continuously held and we had to present medical cases that would be questioned at great length to explain what we did. Everyone was denigrated for errors of omission or inadequate treatment. One conference we attended was for the surgery department and the physician in charge was the department chairman. A nasty person is an understatement. He literally degraded all the interns and residents presenting cases. The man was an extremely handsome fellow that earned him the nickname Hollywood Bob. A year after I finished my surgical rotation, he was arrested and indicted for stealing money from the hospital and was sent to prison.

I met my wife Jeanette during my first year of residency via a mutual friend to be explained in the next chapter. Soon after we started dating, she would bring food to me at the hospital for dinner when I was on call. The hospital food was terrible. This always included a large double chocolate malted which would energize and get me through the long nights on call. The funny thing was as she delivered the food, the malted would spill. We did everything we could do to prevent that from happening to no avail.

I hated living in Brooklyn. I lived there during the wars between the Gambino and Columbo families and other mafia groups. The American Italian club was one block from our apartment. They were murdering each other in the streets. Every few weeks you would find chalk outlines of people who were killed in the streets and on the side-walks. Very scary place to live!

One night when I was assigned to the emergency room they brought in a stabbing victim. Soon after his arrival there was a dis-turbance in the waiting room just outside the emergency room door. A gang of thugs at-tempted to steal the patients motor bike, and they arrived at the emergency after a fight to finish him off. They tried to forcibly enter the emergency after overpowering the se-curity guard. We promptly called the police and all of us barricaded the door until they arrived. This was another HAPPY Brooklyn experience.

Another interesting episode involved the arrival of a patient who apparently had a heart attack. He was middle aged and was essen-tially dead on arrival. No-one attempted to resuscitate him. For some reason something told me to administer CPR. Within a few minutes his heart began beating again and upon seeing what had happened the staff came to my assistance. He came back to life awake and alert. I visited him over the next week or two and he insisted on giving everybody a $ 100.00 bill for saving his life. He was discharged after three weeks. A brief time after that, he again arrived at the hospital after suffering another heart attack but this time did not survive.

In my mind it amazes me how medicine has evolved in treating many illnesses. A patient with a heart attack was required to be hospitalized for no less than three weeks. The first week was spent in the cardiac care unit, the second week in a stepdown unit with a heart monitor and the third week on a regular patient floor before being discharged. Today heart attack patients are discharged after only a few days. Truly amazing!

I must describe to you another very interesting patient. A teenage girl was admitted to my service with a tentative diagnosis of a drug overdose. She was known to use drugs previously. We were told that she had gone to bed and was found unconscious. Lab studies were ordered. When I examined her for the first time, I noticed one of her pupils was markedly dilated. If this had been a drug overdose both pupils would react the same way. I immediately ordered a Neurological consult and it was determined that she had suffered a stroke. She never awoke and died and on autopsy it was revealed that she had a ruptured brain aneurysm which could not be treated.

When I was in my residency, they developed renal dialysis machines. Our hospital received two for inpatient treatment. There were none developed yet for outpatient care. Patients would die from renal failure because there was no way to cleanse their blood. There were many patients that died because of this. With only two machines available we would make rounds and decide who the healthiest ones were and select them for treatment. We were forced to allow the others to die. If there was anything you could say about dying from renal disease is that it is a peaceful death, no pain involved. You just went to sleep. Today, dialysis treatment centers are everywhere, and people are not denied care.

Another surprising event involved the attempted car theft of my wife's 10 year - old car with 85,000 miles and a rusted body. While living in Brooklyn we felt secure that the last car anyone would want to steal would be hers. We never gave it a second thought. One day after I returned home Jeanette was not there, which was unusual. After an extended period of time, she called me to tell me she was at the police station. WHY? Because one of the students at the Junior High School where she taught was arrested for attempting to steal her car. She filed a police report. We do not know what happened to the student.

Parking in Brooklyn on the street was an absolute nightmare. Every day you had restricted parking for street cleaning. One night I parked outside the hospital in what I thought would be a safe place. There were no restrictive signs. The next day I found a parking ticket on my car. I lived in Brooklyn for five years and NEVER got a parking ticket. I decided to take pictures of where I parked, and like Clarence Darrow, I went into a hearing room to appeal my case and not have to pay a hefty fine. When my case was heard, I was called upon to plead my case. They refused my claim and refused to cancel the ticket. As I got up to leave the hearing room, several people also got up and left. I was wearing my hospital whites to the hearing instead of street clothes. Outside the room the people who left told me that if I could not beat the ticket, there was no way they had a chance. We all paid our debt to society.

Three of our favorite places to eat were at Nathan's Hot Dog stand in Coney Island, the Roll N Roaster in Sheepshead Bay, and Juniors on Ocean Parkway. All three restaurants exist today in the same locations. In fact, the Roll N Roaster opened about 1971 when my wife and I began dating. When we went back to New York a few years ago we revisited all of them.

The episode I am going to describe involved the death of one of the patients I was covering overnight for another doctor in training. It left an indelible impression and to this day I will never forget it and what affect it had in affecting my care of all future patients. It is amazing what occurs and how it affects all future things. The patient was an elderly female who was admitted to the hospital with a very high blood sugar. Based on the high sugar level, her doctor prescribed large doses of insulin to get it under control. After a few days, she was ready for discharge

Nathan's Hot Dog Stand

Roll N Roaster

Juniors Restaurant

the next day. I was on call that night and received a call to come to the ward because the patient lost consciousness. When I arrived, I promptly ordered a stat blood sugar and found it was in the single digits. I promptly pumped in as much sugar as I could, but to no avail and she died on the morning she was to be discharged. Just heartbreaking. How did the blood sugar get so low? Her doctor was heading home and upon checking her medical record found a blood sugar report that was high. He did not check the date it was done and it was somehow placed near the beginning of the chart. In haste he ordered insulin which resulted in her death. HE DID NOT CHECK THE DATE WHEN THE REPORT WAS DONE, which was a few days earlier on her admission to the hospital. This episode totally depressed me. To this day, when I look at lab reports I always check the dates they were done.

While I was at Brookdale Medical Center during my second year of Internal Medicine Residency, I visited the Emergency Room one evening. They brought in a young prostitute to be treated for a serious infection. She was given a Penicillin injection and immediately suffered an anaphylactic reaction. I was entertaining subspecialty training in Allergy & Immunology at that time. I knew that if you did not treat an anaphylactic reaction with enough epinephrine the patient would die. None of the physicians knew what to do. The patient broke out in huge hives with intense flushing of the skin and was gasping for air as she started to lose consciousness. I immediately administered a full milliliter of epinephrine, enough to kill a healthy adult. I had to administer another almost 2 milliliters of epinephrine, and we were very lucky she survived. This was the worst case of anaphylaxis I have ever seen since that episode. She would have died if I had not been there. She was one very lucky woman. This occurred one year before I entered my Allergy Fellowship training program.

Another major event occurred again when I was visiting the ER at Brookdale. Two police officers were brought for treatment after being attacked a few blocks away while they were driving slowly in their patrol car. They both had multiple shotgun wounds. Brownsville, Brooklyn is where the hospital is located which had the highest crime rate in the city. While driving slowly they passed a man in a trench coat. As soon as they passed him, he pulled out a shotgun and fired multiple times into their car. Both officers survived and it was disclosed that the two officers were brothers. The car they were driving was riddled with shotgun pellets. Police Commissioner Murphy came to the ER and visited them. On the front page of the New York Post, Times, and other papers the episode was reported. Pictures of the riddled car were shown. I still have the news articles of that incident. Because of what happened, New York City decided that no relatives are allowed together when patrolling the city.

They built a highrise residence for the doctors at the hospital. There were many incidents of snipers firing into the building. It was like a war zone there and you always had to look over your shoulder.

As I entered my second year of Internal Medicine Residency, I was undecided as to subspecialty training in Cardiology or the field of Allergy and Immunology. To help me decide, I concentrated on Cardiology training for ten months. The program director was Alan F. Lyon, M.D. an internationally recognized authority on electrocardiography. Patients traveled from around the world to become his patients. Once a year he traveled to visit and treat Halie Salassie, the Emperor of Ethiopia, until in 1975 he died in a coup d'état at the age of 83 in August, 1975.

During my training at Maimonides as well as Brookdale hospital, it became obvious that the cardiologists were frequently called to the hospital to treat patients. Many of them told me that their family life was continually disrupted and suggested to me that I avoid that specialty. My interests turned to Allergy. There was an Allergy Training program at Long Island College Hospital in Brooklyn. The program director was Larry Chiaramonte, M.D. I made an appointment to interview with him. There was an opening for one new Fellow the following year. About this time the Allergy programs were becoming combined programs. Previously, the programs were either adult or pediatric. He was interested in bringing an Internist into his Pediatric program and welcomed me. At that time his department was researching allergic sensitivity to cockroach as it related to severe asthma in ghetto children. They proved a definite correlation and when ghetto children were treated with cockroach extract there was a marked decrease in severity and frequency of asthma attacks.

During my two - year Allergy training program I published a research paper titled *"Comparison of an Electronic Spirometer with a Pediatric Wright Peak Flow Meter and their Relationship to Clinical Symptomatology in Asthmatic Children"*. It was published in the Journal of Asthma Research, volume 13, 1976 – Issue 3. It was published online on July 2, 2009.

A tragedy struck my family in the early 1980's. My sister in law Christine was murdered on their farm in Sussex, New Jersey. They were boarding horses at the time and one afternoon she went to put eye drops in one of the horses. In the barn she was shot once in the head execution style by an unknown person and died instantly. Sussex was a very small farming community in northwest New Jersey not far from High Point, New Jersey. At High Point there is a small park and a large monument. The monument demarks the place where New York, Pennsylvania, and New Jersey meet at one point and you can look into each state.

After she was murdered it was found that the person who murdered her was James Hampton a career criminal in jail most of his life. He was wanted in Missouri for the murder of another woman who he kidnapped and tried to hold for ransom. He told her husband that he had a police scanner and if he notified the authorities, he would murder her. The police were notified, and he murdered her. He was a drifter and ended up in New Jersey. He got a job as a handyman in a small church. He somehow ended up in Sussex and lived in the woods at the back of my brother's property. He would return to the church as well to work. His plan was to kidnap Chris and hold her for ransom, but because she resisted him, he killed her on the spot. A day or two later, Hampton called my brother on the phone requesting money for information about the murder. Unbeknown to him, all phone calls were being traced and were made from a telephone booth across the street from the Rectory. *America's Most Wanted* show came to Sussex and did a one-half hour episode in hopes of finding the murderer. After it aired, the priest at the small church saw it and suspected Hampton. He notified police of his suspicion and they tried to arrest him. As they approached him, he took out a hand gun and shot himself in the head. The gun he used was the same one he used to kill Christine. He survived his self-inflicted wound. Missouri was notified and wanted him returned there for trial first. The death penalty was allowed there, but not in New Jersey. He was found guilty of murdering the first woman and sentenced to death, which was carried out about one year later. His last words before dying were "take the phone off the hook." He did not want the governor to call and stay his execution. The whole episode was surreal. It still hurts these many years later when I relive it in my mind and numerous newspaper articles were written detailing the whole episode. She was only 44 years old when she died.

One winter while living in Brooklyn, we had an ice storm which covered our cars in ice with frigid temperatures. My wife had parked her car across the street from mine. We both went to our respective cars to remove the ice. Soon after we started, she told me that she had broken her windshield while using a hammer to clear off the ice. I was really upset and yelled at her for doing such a stupid thing. Then I admitted to her that I had broken the rearview mirror on my car using a screwdriver to remove the ice. Needless to say, this cemented our decision to leave the northeast and settle in Florida.

During the holidays one year we decided to take a trip to the Eastern tip of Long Island to Montauk Point. Let me tell you, that was a big mistake. The day we arrived on the beach there was an ice and snow storm with sub-freezing temperatures. The experience of being on a snow-covered beach in a storm is something I would not want to repeat.

One day while driving down the Westside Highway, there was a large British flatbed warship (SS Hermes) docked at one of the piers. My wife decided we should take a tour of the boat. We were a day late and all of the tours had ended. There was no way my wife would take no for an answer. She got on the phone and was able to speak to Commander Bond. She explained that I was a physician and would like to see the medical facilities on the boat. He told her that he would be off the boat the next day, but Lieutenant Corey would be happy to give us a tour. We were met by him and he took us all over the boat. Also, on that day, there was a ceremony and we met Vanessa Redgrave who was on board.

We invited Lieutenant Corey on a tour and ferry ride to Staten Island. It was a beautiful July day. On the ride to Staten Island we

Staten Island Ferry

suggested his best pictures of Manhattan would be on the return trip. As luck would have it, on the trip back, large storm clouds blew in from New Jersey. It was a violent fast - moving storm with golf sized hail and sleet. Everyone had to abandon deck. It was very scary and sudden with high wind. This happened in July. In my life, I never experienced such a storm. Unfortunately, the Lieutenant did not get the pictures we wanted him to take.

Soon after it was decided that I would need to have four impacted wisdom teeth removed. It was absolutely terrible! They were to be removed using local an-aesthetic, with me fully awake. The oral surgeon had a terrible time removing them. Despite not feeling any pain, I do remember my gums being cut and the cracking of each tooth while being removed. After removing the first one he advised me to have the other three removed as an inpatient at the hospital. I told him it all had to be done then and now because there was no way I would schedule another day. I was sutured and unable to eat any solids for a week, and sustained myself with liquids and puree. I lost a lot of weight. I only weighed 155 lbs. before the surgery.

While in residency training, I was entitled to a medical meeting with all expenses paid. We decided to go to Denver and while there visited Pikes Peak. Upon entering the park and the road leading to the summit, we came upon a rock store full of all types of geodes and other mineral containing rocks. We befriended the owners and they invited us to a dinner show. It was wonderful, and we mingled with other locals from the area.

We entered the park during off season. We were told that there were bears near the large lake at the foot of the mountain. As we drove, we encountered the most beautiful lake surrounded by mountains. We decide to stop and walk towards the water to take pictures. While taking pictures, we heard a rustling in the woods close by and growling. I don't think we ever ran as fast as we did for the safety of our car. We were very lucky since we were told that bears could easily outrun any human.

We drove up the narrow mountain road to reach the top of the mountain. Two things stopped us. The first was the fact that an early winter storm closed the last mile. Second, the air was so thin that neither of us could breathe properly so we retreated to a lower level.

On the way out of the park we stopped at the rock shop to say goodbye. My wife was a middle school science teacher and taught some geology. The couple insisted on giving us a large number of rocks to take home. We did not think far enough ahead to realize they were very, very heavy. Would the plane be able to take off?? At the airport we needed help getting to the ticket counter. The porter lifted the bag, stopped and looked at us, and asked "DO YOU HAVE ROCKS IN HERE?!?" Very funny. Alas, the plane took off and all was ok.

On the drive to Pike's Peak we stopped at sights along the way. We visited the Cave of the Winds, a popular geological site. We took a tour into the chilly cave. Unfortunately, the ceiling was low, and my wife suffered a cut on her forehead with a lot of bleeding. We were able to apply a bandage and avoided using sutures. As we continued to drive, we had a flat tire. A Colorado State Trooper stopped to help us. He saw the bandage on my wife's head and looked at me, as if I caused the injury. He mentioned to us that

Canon City was the next city we would pass through. He mentioned that Canon City was home to the Colorado State Penitentiary, and that they gave tours of the facility, which is a Maximum-Security prison. They also had a gift shop in the entrance and sold products created by the inmates. Whatever was sold was credited to their personal accounts. The prison was built against a mountain wall. The other three sides had two very tall chain linked fences with barbed wire and guard towers. It really looked ominous, and scary, but we were young and stupid and decided to visit.

We walked up to the entry gate and a guard in one of the towers asked us what we wanted. We told him we were there to take a tour. He opened the first tall gate and beckoned us in. Then after it closed behind us, he opened the second gate. We walked into reception and to the right was the gift shop. The most beautiful items were ornate jewel cases. We are sorry we did not purchase one when we had the chance.

In the reception area we were required to check in all our personal items before the tour. That concerned me. An inmate on good

Colorado State Penitentiary

behavior was selected to be our tour guide. He was serving a life sentence for murdering his girlfriend. That made me feel really secure. There were no prison guards with us as we entered the main building. It was the most unbelievable tour we ever took. Beyond awesome! We were taken to all areas i.e. sleeping quarters, dining room, kitchen facilities, bathrooms, outside yard for exercise, etc. What was scary was that all the prisoners were free at that time in all those areas. The prison guards were visible in the high guard towers, but we had no protection. We felt very uncomfortable walking amongst the prisoners who gave us a good looking over. Lucky for us the tour was uneventful and although frightening, we were not threatened by anybody. We could have been held hostage. It was truly scary. We collected our possessions and safely departed. A few months after we visited, a riot broke out and several people were injured and died. From that point on, all prison tours were stopped. We were very lucky.

A couple of years later, when we were visiting San Francisco, on the way into the city from the airport there was a turn off for San Quentin Prison. Of course, we were curious, and my wife wanted to take a tour. We drove up to the main gate. Again, high double fencing and guard towers. We walked up to the entrance and the guard asked what we wanted. My wife told him we wanted to take a tour. His reply was the only way in was if we were put there. That was laughable!

When I was in my Residency training, we were required to wear neckties with our whites. Most of the time, I refused and was admonished for not wearing one. One of the reasons I decided to move to Florida was because that was never a requirement. Several years after I went into private-practice, studies involving hospital acquired infections showed that wearing ties would transmit infections to patients, and everyone stopped wearing ties in the hospital. That vindicated me.

CHAPTER 10
Marriage and Honeymoon

This chapter by far is the most emotional for me because it describes how I met the LOVE OF MY LIFE. After 48 years of marriage my love for her has grown to the point that we are one and continue to enjoy all the things that life has to offer. She has supported me in everything that I have done. She has created so many special moments. I am so happy that she picked me to be that one special person in her life. I only wish I could please her more and be able to express my deep love for her.

When people ask me what makes a successful marriage, my response is always that I am still madly in love with her and she tolerates me.

It was during my Medical Internship at Maimonides Medical Center in Brooklyn, New York that we first met. A mutual friend was instrumental in introducing us to each other. His name was Stanley August, M.D. a Pediatric Resident at the same hospital. One day while I was on rotation through the Emergency Room, he handed me a piece of paper with her name and phone number. He thought we would be a good match. I never called her and threw the paper away. A few weeks later he asked me if I ever called her and I told him I did not. On the spot he wrote her name and phone number down again, handed it to me, and made me promise that I would call her. I DID MAKE THAT CALL. It was challenging for me for three reasons. First of all, I was not the most social person in the world and was very introverted and shy. Secondly, I never had a blind date before, and thirdly, I never called a total stranger to have a conversation. You have no idea how hard it was for me to make that call. It scared the hell out of me, but I did make that call, and to this very day I will never regret having done it.

When I called her, I mentioned that Stanley had given me her number. We spoke for

Jeanette engagement

some time, but I have absolutely no memory of what I said or what we discussed. The result of that call was that we had our first date. She took a chance on me and I am so happy she did. She was a middle school Biology teacher with a Master's Degree and was very intelligent and easy to talk to.

On our first date, I brought her a bouquet of red roses. Her mother answered the door and asked if she could take them and put them in a vase. I told her no thanks, that I wanted to give them to her daughter. When I first set eyes on my date, I was totally unprepared for the most beautiful girl I had ever seen. She was beyond beautiful. I later learned that she came in second in a beauty pageant in Brighton Beach. I had a loss for words and for me it was very awkward. Our first date consisted of having dinner at a Chinese restaurant followed by a movie. The meal we had at the restaurant was an experience I will never forget. I had no idea what she liked and asked her twice what she would like to eat. She told me that whatever I order for myself would be fine. There were things that I would eat regularly including pork fried rice, egg rolls, spare ribs etc. She seemed to be satisfied with that and I never gave it a second thought. It seemed that when we did things during dating, she always deferred decisions to me - "Anything you want dear". After we were married, everything was switched around. Now it is "anything I want dear". Kind of funny how things changed.

We went to see the movie *Plaza Suite* with Walter Matthau. It was a funny movie and I of course have a copy of it.

At the end of the date I knew beyond a doubt that I would marry her. As insecure and as shy as I was, I just knew it. It was truly love at first sight. I gave her a goodnight kiss and asked to see her again and she agreed. I was so excited and happy. I told her that the next weekend I was flying to Paris, France for a long weekend but that I would like to see her in two weeks and she agreed.

This is where things became really complicated. I was dating another girl, an accomplished pianist. I had been seeing her on a regular basis. One of the major Airlines was running special deep discounts for travel to Paris. It was only a 4- day trip, but was very inexpensive. Her uncle was the Public Relations Director for the Lido night club. So, to make a long story short we brought tickets to go. We were to leave the next weekend after my first date with Jeanette.

Just before I left on the trip to Paris, I spoke to Jeanette almost daily. Two days or so before I left, Jeanette told me she wanted to meet me at the airport to see me off. Thank G-d she told me and did not surprise me. I had to tell her I was going to Paris with a girl and the circumstances surrounding it. I told her that I wanted to see her when I got back. This episode could have been a deal breaker for us, but she accepted it and we moved forward with our relationship upon my return.

The trip to Paris was exciting. It was my first trip there. My girlfriend's uncle placed me in a French Hotel with a wire cage elevator, and no one spoke a word of English. My girlfriend stayed with them. The second morning upon awakening and getting dressed my shoes were missing. I was able to speak to someone at the desk with broken English. It is customary in French hotels that if you leave your shoes on the floor, they are taken away to be polished. Another interesting fact - Education is free to everyone, including college, graduate school, medical school etc. The only requirement is that you must pass special tests for entrance. A great deal if you are a French citizen.

Her uncle took us all around Paris for sightseeing. The highlight of that weekend was a visit to the Lido club. Her uncle sat us front row center for the show. The Lido Club is known for their spectacular productions and this was by far no exception. There is nothing like this in the states. When the show started the lights were dimmed, the curtain was raised, and a team of galloping horses raced from the back of the stage to the audience on a very large stage. They stopped the horses only a few feet from us. It scared the hell out of us and I will never forget it.

When we flew back from Paris as we were passing through U.S. Customs, they looked at our passport and could not believe we flew to Paris for just a few days. Since that trip, airfares were never that low again.

Once back in the states, Jeanette and I began to seriously date. I could not see enough of her and I was totally immersed in her persona.

Jeanette & Seth

Just a note of interest and surprise - Stanley August who was instrumental in setting up the blind date did not know that both Jeanette and myself have birthdays in the month of AUGUST and that my middle name is STANLEY. How unusual is that?

Another funny episode occurred during our relationship when Jeanette decided to buy new car mats. She went to an auto supply store and after a few days we decided that we really did not need them. We went back to the store to return them and they told us we could not return them because they were dirty. My wife told the clerk that she would wash them for him and took them into an adjoining room and using soap cleaned the mats. He then issued a credit for them. I observed all-of this looking on in amazement.

On one occasion we decided to dine at a highly rated restaurant just outside of New York city. The directions we were given directed us to look for a tree in the middle of the road. As we drove to our destination, we found ourselves in the middle of a heavily wooded area. How were we to find that specific tree? Alas, suddenly it was there. For some reason they cleared the woods and left one tree standing IN THE MIDDLE OF THE ROAD. One would never believe it.

After seven months of dating we decided to get married. The ceremony and reception were held at Tamcrest Country Club in Alpine, New Jersey near Fort Lee, New Jersey. The best party I ever attended. Rabbi Rothstein conducted the service. I later learned that Rabbi Rothstein was Buddy Hackett's Rabbi and he officiated at his funeral in California. Buddy owned a home in Fort Lee, New Jersey on Bluff Road. The home previously belonged to Albert Anastasia (murder incorporated) a prominent mobster. He purchased the home for $ 5 million dollars at auction. My father engaged a Society Orchestra with violins, my wife's favorite instrument. Our song was Lara's Theme from Doctor Zhivago. It was such a wonderful evening and when it was finally over, I cried in joy for receiving the greatest gift I ever received, my lovely wife. Was all this really happening to me? I pinched myself more than once.

My future wife was almost late for the wedding. After leaving home for the ceremony, she realized she forgot her shoes and had to return home to get them. She also missed

Miss Diamond Is Bride Of Dr. Seth Schurman

Diamond, daughter of Mr. and Mrs. David Diamond of 2250 E. 4th St., Brooklyn, N.Y., was united in marriage with Dr. Seth Schurman, son of Mr. and Mrs. Abe Schurman of 598 20th Ave., Paterson, at Tamcrest Country Club here.

Rabbi Solomon Rothstein of the Fort Lee Jewish Center officiated. A reception followed.

Mrs. Stuart Selkin of Brooklyn was honor attendant. The bride's nieces, Amy and Ilene Diamond of Brooklyn, were flower grils.

Dr. Alan Schurman of Chicago served as his brother's best man. Dr. Selkin ushered with Floyd Bellet of Bloomfield, Marvin Schurman of Totowa, Seymour Rosenteur of Fair Lawn, and Franklin Pearl and Edward Roth, both of Brooklyn.

Mrs. Schurman received B.S. and M.A. degrees from 'New York University. She is a science teacher at Junior High School 43 in Brooklyn.

Her husband holds an M.D. degree from Chicago Medical School and is a first-year res-

MRS. SETH SCHURMAN

ident in internal medicine at Maimonides Hospital, Brooklyn. He is the grandson of the late Mr. and Mrs. Samuel Rosenteur of Paterson.

The newlyweds left for a honeymoon trip to Jamaica.

Wedding Announcement

Wedding Picture

Wedding Picture

the Hors d'oeuvres because they were having problems attaching the train to her wedding dress.

Funny aside - our first night was memorable for many reasons I cannot divulge. We had opened a bottle of wine, specifically Beaujolais Superieur Vintage 1971, a Monsieur Henri Selection and had partially recorked it. After consummating our relationship almost immediately, the cork popped off the bottle with a loud noise. It was shocking at the time. I saved that empty bottle, and to this day it sits on the mantle in our bedroom. What timing! We both popped our cork at the same time.

We left the next day for Jamaica for two weeks. The first week was spent at the Half Moon Hotel in Montego Bay. We rented a cottage with a private pool and a gardener. He would climb the coconut palm trees to get us coconuts with his bare feet. Then would slice off the ends so we could enjoy fresh coconut milk. The cottage consisted of two - units side by side. We became friends with the other couple from Sicily. They spoke limited English but enough for us to get by. They were a lovely couple several years older than

Beaujolais Superieur 1971

us. When our week was over, we bid them a goodbye and they invited us to visit them in Sicily. We were married on February 26, 1972. As luck would have it, that summer we took a three - week American Express package tour to Europe. One week in Rome, one week in Paris and one week in London. It cost us only $ 1,000.00 for each week, including round trip air, hotels, transportation and most meals. One might say it was an incredible deal. While in Rome we telephoned our Sicilian friends to say hello. Unfortunately, they were a distance away, so we could not visit them. We had an interpreter help us.

My wife wanted to play tennis at the hotel. I was so exhausted from the trip that I was unable to play so she paid hotel staff to play tennis with her.

The Half Moon Hotel had a large buffet on a patio overlooking the ocean. The food was excellent. One night we were seated at a table next to a three - foot stone wall. As we were eating, we were startled by a rodent of some type running back and forth along the wall, not more than a few feet away from us. Shocking to say the least! We quickly took our feet off the ground when it ran by. No-one else at adjoining tables reacted to its presence. We called over the maître d'. He was a large German man with a thick German accent. We told him about the rodent. His answer in thick German was "ve vill exterminate it in ze morning". This ruined our romantic meal under a full moon.

After one week we had a driver take us to the Tower Isle Hotel in Ocho Rios a distance away. It was a memorable trip because every few miles he would stop at a home for a few minutes while we waited in the car which was very unusual. After this happened a few times I asked him what was going on. He told me he was stopping for liquid nourishment on the way, specifically rum. I told him under no circumstance was he to stop until we got to our hotel.

Another scary episode while in Ocho Rios occurred when we were in a taxi cab. We were driving in the downtown area when all of a sudden, a riot broke out around us. People were streaming into the street preventing our passage. They were carrying poles, garden tools, and other items. We were in the car and they were all over us, on the hood, the roof etc. We were scared for our lives. It was then explained to us that an election on the Island had just occurred and they were celebrating the election of the new leader of Jamaica, Mr. Mann. Not to be believed!

We enjoyed a visit to Dunn's River Falls outside Ocho Rios. The most beautiful waterfall with a lot of rocks and tropical vegetation. The water was frigid and so unbelievably cold! All the tourists climbed up the rocks and nearly froze to death. A few years after we were there, they prevented anybody from climbing the falls because the water was polluted.

Another trip we took was Rafting on the Rio Grande River. It had grade 1 to 2 rapids. We were placed on small wooden rafts (without seatbelts) and our guide would stand in front and with a bamboo pole guide us down the river. It was a beautiful trip but for one exception. Along the way as we passed small villages, the children waded out into the river to beg for money.

Back in Brooklyn we settled into married life. She wanted to decorate the apartment. She decided that the bathroom would have zebra striped wallpaper. Not only that, but the floor and ceiling would have the same paper as well as the toilet seat cover. You felt that you were in Africa whenever you went to the bathroom!

The first piece of art we purchased was that of a man embracing a woman. We continued purchasing art from around the world.

First Art Purchase

WELCOME TO
KEESLER AIR FORCE BASE

CHAPTER 11
Air Force

My wife and I experienced two scary incidents prior to leaving New York city
for my assignment in the Air Force. Both occurred within two weeks of each other and
were similar. During the first incident, we
were driving north on the Eastside Highway
in Manhattan. As we were driving, we noticed
several police cars with lights flashing on the
west side of the highway. They were chasing
a man crossing the highway directly in front
of us. I jammed on my brakes to avoid hitting

him when he crossed in front of our car. The police close behind with guns drawn. We were driving a Dodge Dart Sport car and I told my wife to get down as much as possible. I am 6'4" tall and could not get down. There was a man directly in front of our car without a police uniform and with a gun in his hand. I told my wife if he turned towards me with the gun, I would run him over. Luckily, he did not and turned out to be an undercover officer. About two weeks later, the second incident occurred and we were again driving on the Eastside Highway. We had to stop while police again were chasing a man across the highway and we both agreed IT WAS TIME TO LEAVE NEW YORK.

I entered the Air Force in the summer of 1975 and was stationed in Biloxi, Mississippi. I was a cultural shock moving there from New York City. The city is located directly on the Gulf of Mexico and they only flew Confederate Flags along the coast. Everyone used CB radios and the accents in Biloxi were so difficult to understand. We lived there for two years and left still not able to understand their accent.

We lived off base in the Oakwood Apartments directly across highway 90 from the Gulf. We had a swimming pool just outside our door. The city suffered a direct hit from a major hurricane years before resulting in the destruction of large mansions located directly across highway 90 from the gulf. All that were left were concrete slabs with steps. While I lived there for two years, we were threatened by one hurricane which at the last minute turned and headed to Mobile, Alabama. We were evacuated to the Air Force base during the storm. We visited Biloxi twice since we left, and the mansions were rebuilt where they had been before. On August 29, 2005, Hurricane Katrina a cat 5 hurricane made a direct hit on New Orleans and Biloxi received a lot of damage. This time the destruction extended into land by several city blocks, destroying everything in its path. It destroyed all the places we frequented. It destroyed the Oakwood apartment complex and our favorite restaurants. Revisiting Biloxi following the storm brought me to tears. The Air Force base survived.

One of our best restaurants we ate at often managed to survive. Mary Mahoney. It is located behind the Marina downtown and somehow managed to survive. It is still open to this day. We knew Mary and after her passing her son took over to keep it open. When

Mary Mahoney's
Old French House
Restaurant and
Slave Quarters
Lounge. Built 1737.

Lunch served from
11 A.M.
Dinners served from
5 P.M.
Lounge opens 11 A.M.

Mary Mahoney Restaurant

you walk into the restaurant, on the wall a line was drawn to delineate how much water flooded the restaurant. After Hurricane Katrina, the water line was far higher than previous hurricanes

We used to go to New Orleans on weekends to get away and explore the city. We went to Mardi Gras one year and that will be the last time we will ever do it. It was like rioting in the streets. We felt very unsafe, and we left soon after the parade started. There is a lot of crime and very little security.

When we first moved to Biloxi, we were introduced to tree roaches. My first encounter with one was while I was sitting on the edge of my bed, and one flew past my head to land on the headboard. It was very large, resembled a roach, and flew. Being bug phobic, I was ready to pack up and go AWOL from the air force. I somehow was able to coexist with them while I lived in Biloxi.

My wife enrolled in Lamaze classes prior to the birth of our first child. They were held at a local church nearby. Previous experiences with tree roaches revealed that they hate exposure to light. When it gets dark, they come out to "play". One night at the church we were all on the floor with our pillows practicing breathing exercises. That night a storm turned off the power and the large room became pitch black. We yelled to everybody to get off the floor immediately and climb on the tables nearby. When the lights turned on a short time later, there were a large number of roaches coming out and they immediately fled back to their hiding places. All the women were screaming. I vividly remember that night.

Once a year, the Ku Klux Klan would march down Highway 90 in front of our apartment complex, with a full hood and regalia carrying crosses, some of which were burning. The highway was closed, and we watched the spectacle from the safety of our apartment.

While we were in Biloxi, we purchased an 18-foot-Glastron motor boat with a 115HP Mercury outboard motor. A beautiful boat with orange striping. Our neighbor was into boating and helped us with the purchase. The boat cost about $ 3,400.00. Today it would cost over $ 30,000.00. Off the coast from Biloxi was Ship Island, approximately 20 miles away. He decided to help us celebrate

Glastron Motor Boat 18'

our purchase by taking us out to the Island. The day we went, there was a heavy fog and the only way to get to the island was by using our compass. He assured us all would be well. We couldn't even see the bow of the boat and as we moved along, we had to sound our horn to warn other boats about our presence. They did as well, to avoid a collision. We made it safely to and from the island. It was an exciting, scary day!

While in the Air Force, we were visiting Florida to determine where we would like to settle. We were returning to Biloxi on a single lane road in the panhandle which was heavily wooded, pitch black, and in the middle of nowhere. We came upon a serious accident which literally occurred a few minutes before we arrived. It was a grisly scene. A car was trying to pass another and caused a horrific accident. In one of the cars a man was trapped behind the wheel with broken ribs, but was alive and breathing. A woman was thrown out of the car into the woods. It was pitch black. I told my wife to drive the car into the woods so we could determine what the situation was. The woman was unconscious without a heartbeat. I immediately administered CPR to her and was able to restart her heart. On examination her arm was broken and bent backward. Literally not attached completely to her body. Paramedics finally came. I had to hold her arm in place until we got her to the hospital. To my knowledge she survived. We needed to get back to Biloxi, and left soon after she was admitted to the hospital.

My first daughter, Ava, was born at Keesler Air Force Base on June 24, 1976. It was unusual because when my wife went into labor, the hospital lost all power. Dr. Hemsley, her obstetrician, examined her using a flashlight until she finally delivered. My daughter saw the light of day soon after delivery. Her birth weight was 8 lbs. and 1 ounce. She was post mature at delivery with a full head of hair.

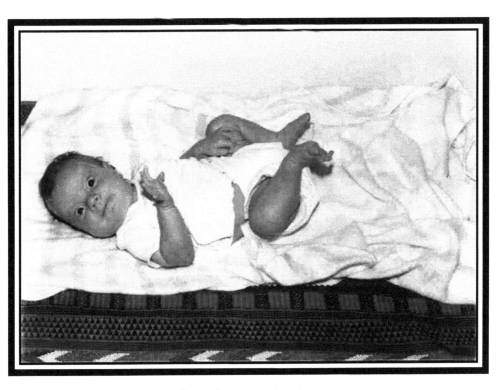

Ava born 6/24/76

CHAPTER 12
Lessons Learned

- Writing this book was easy to do because I was completely immersed in something that I knew better than anything else, ME.

- It took me almost two years from start to finish. I enjoyed the entire process and intend to continue writing. I learned that it will take two or three books to complete the entire process. I invite you to follow me as I describe my worldly travels, many celebrity encounters, and other

  - personal experiences, including some very interesting encounters in my medical practice.

- I learned that writing this book helps me cement all the memories. My mind feels less cluttered, knowing that I will never forget and can always return to this book to remember them.

- Reinforcing memories by applying pen to paper is so gratifying.

- Never hit a female at any age, even at age 4, with a shovel.

- Breaking a wild horse taught me to never give up on anything in the future. You will succeed if you are persistent in what you do.

- Never drink milk directly from a cow, or risk exposure to Brucellosis.

- Avoid eating crab apples at all costs. They are a very strong laxative.

- Never allow giant bullfrogs to run loose in a hotel lobby.

- Never go fishing especially at 5 AM. Haven't gone fishing since.

- Never play in the woods during a thunder and lightning storm.

- Never light a firecracker while holding it.

- At bullfights, always sit on the shady side of the bull ring.

- Never have sex with an animal.

- Pollution is destroying the environment.

- Not buying land at $ 50.00 an acre on the Las Vegas strip was a big mistake.

- Never fall face first into wet cement.

- If water temperature is under 85 degrees, do not swim in it.

- Never shine a flashlight on a couple having intimate relations.

- Never start smoking.

- Let a dentist remove a tooth.

- Never wake up a sleep walker.

- Do not eat raw eggs and risk getting Salmonella poisoning.

- Never speed during a rain storm. The car will hydroplane.

- Read the entire document before taking a test.

- Delivering a baby is not that difficult.

- After examining a patient, make sure you have the entire stethoscope with you before leaving the room.

- Never boil a live lobster.

- Always expect the unexpected.

- Before prescribing any medication, one must review the patient's record and the lab reports must be the latest and up to date.

- When treating an anaphylactic reaction, one must err on the side of overtreatment to prevent death.

- Never use a hammer or screwdriver to remove ice from a windshield or side mirror.

- Do not have four impacted wisdom teeth removed surgically at the same time as an outpatient. I regret making that decision.

- Do not take a tour of a maximum-security prison unaccompanied by a guard. I won't do that again.

- Never approach any prison asking for a tour.

- Shoes left on the floor of a French Hotel will automatically be taken away to be polished.

- In France, all education is free including graduate and medical school, if you have the necessary grades.

- NEVER HITCHHIKE.

Illustrations

** Paterson, New Jersey - childhood home

** Abe and Bea (2)

** Declaration of Intention – Ellis Island

** William Schurman (Prince Edward Island)

** Melody Country Club - Liberty, New York

** 1953 Cadillac

** Triangle Diner – Liberty, New York

** Celebrity Autographs – Las Vegas & Los Angeles, California (2)

** Yosemite National Park – Fire Fall

** Garfield Grant Hotel – Long Branch, New Jersey

** Colony Surf Club (West End Casino) – Long Branch, New Jersey (2)

** Train Station – Long Branch, New Jersey

** Boardwalk – Asbury Park, New Jersey

** Merry-Go-Round – Asbury Park, New Jersey

** Merry-Go-Round (One black horse) – Asbury Park, New Jersey

** Palace Amusements (Ferris Wheel) – Asbury Park, New Jersey

** Swan Boat Ride – Asbury Park, New Jersey

** The Berkeley-Carteret Hotel (1920) – Asbury Park, New Jersey

** Monte Carlo Pool – Asbury Park, New Jersey

** The Stone Pony (Bruce Springsteen) – Asbury Park, New Jersey

** Original Dave & Evelyn's Sea Food – Belmar, New Jersey

** Cornerstone Time Capsule Letter 1962 – Bloomfield, New Jersey

** Seth Court – Staten Island, New Jersey

** Seth Court Apartments

** Lou Costello childhood home – Paterson, New Jersey

** Jan's Ice Cream Parlor (Kitchen Sink) – Fair Lawn, New Jersey

** Tree Tavern Restaurant – Paterson, New Jersey

** Silk Mill – Paterson, New Jersey

** Ice Delivery Man – Paterson, New Jersey

** Marble Statue – Paterson, New Jersey (2)

** Regency Transistor Radio

** Brownie Hawkeye Camera Flash Model

** Eastside High School – Paterson, New Jersey

** Cook County Hospital – Chicago, Illinois

** The Greeks Restaurant – Chicago, Illinois

** 1969 Snow Storm – Chicago, Illinois

** Wedding Night (cork popping) – East Paterson, New Jersey

** Mary Mahoney Restaurant - Biloxi, Mississippi

** Jeanette and Seth Schurman

** Schickhaus Hot Dogs - Long Branch, New Jersey

** Colorado State Penitentiary - Canon City, Colorado

** White Castle Square Hamburgers - Forest Park, Illinois (2)

** Mitchell Park - Milwaukee, Wisconsin (3 Domes) (2)

** Bullring by the Sea - Tijuana, Mexico

** Grammar School # 20 - Paterson, New Jersey

- Nathan's Hot Dogs, Roll N Roaster - Coney Island & Sheepshead Bay
- Juniors Restaurant – Brooklyn, New York
- Café Du Monde - New Orleans, Louisiana
- Staten Island Ferry - New York
- 18' Glastron Boat with a 115HP Mercury Outboard Motor - Biloxi, MS.
- Artwork Statue - Brooklyn, New York
- Las Vegas, Nevada (2)
- Alexander Hamilton Hotel - Paterson, New Jersey
- Bonfire Restaurant - Paterson, New Jersey
- Wedding Photos (2)
- Alan & Seth
- Rutt's Hut - Clifton, New Jersey
- Simca 1000
- Wedding Announcement
- Howard Johnson
- Ava Baby
- Apartments – Long Branch, New Jersey
- Beaujolais Superieur Vintage 1971
- Statue – First Piece of Art

About the Author

I was born at the Passaic General Hospital in Passaic, New Jersey on August 29, 1945. My family moved to Paterson, New Jersey a few years later, where I lived for 20 years before I entered the Chicago Medical School. Upon graduation in 1970, I did a Straight Medical Internship for one year, followed by a two-year Medical Residency, and a two-year Allergy Fellowship Program. I entered the United States Air Force for two years and was Chief of Allergy at Keesler Air Force Base in Biloxi, Mississippi.

Upon completion of my military service, I moved to Fort Myers, Florida to begin my Allergy practice on July 11, 1977. I opened and operate three offices in Fort Myers, Cape Coral, and Naples. I continue in active practice as of this printing. The immense satisfaction I get from practicing my specialty prevents me from considering retirement anytime soon.

I have never written anything of substance before. About two years ago I became motivated to write my life's story. The reason I became motivated is outlined at the beginning of this book. As I continued to write, I found the process to be emotionally satisfying.

I am presently outlining my next book which will take you further along on my life's journey after serving in the Air Force. I suppose I can enter AUTHOR as part of my curriculum vitae. It is fun to be creative as I enter the next CHAPTER (pun intended) of my life.

<u>Seth S. Schurman, M.D.</u>
Physician/Author

CPSIA information can be obtained
at www.ICGtesting.com
Printed in the USA
LVHW072357311021
702073LV00005B/21